British Muslims and the call to global jihad

British Muslims and the call to global jihad

Kylie Baxter

Monash University Press
Clayton

Monash University Press
Building 11
Monash University
Victoria 3800, Australia

www.monash.edu.au/mai

All Monash University Press publications are subject to double blind peer review

© Kylie Baxter 2007

National Library of Australia cataloguing-in-publication data:

Baxter, Kylie.
British Muslims and the call to global Jihad.

Bibliography.
ISBN 9781876924553 (pbk.).

1. Islamic fundamentalism - Great Britain. 2. Islam and politics - Great Britain. 3. Jihad. I. Title. (Series : Islam and Muslim affairs ; 1).

320.5570941

Islam and Muslim Affairs : ISSN 1834 - 6081

Cover design by Emma Fisher.
Printed by BPA Print Group, Melbourne, Australia - www.bpabooks.com

For Angela

Odd Anderson/AFP/Getty Images

Omar Bakri Muhammad addresses a public meeting of al-Muhajiroun.

Author's foreword

This book pivots on the experience of al-Muhajiroun's founder, Omar Bakri Muhammad. I had planned to interview Bakri in London in early July 2005. The terrorist attacks of July 7 made this impossible. After Bakri's departure from the United Kingdom, an interview seemed unlikely. However, an opportunity emerged and I met with Bakri in Lebanon in July 2007. By this stage, this book was already completed. In the July 2007 interview, Bakri provided a substantially different version of his own life story. As is acknowledged, a range of strategic reasons may well have influenced his presentation. Bakri is a skilled media operator. He is a man who shot to infamy as a result of his willingness to be a lightening rod for Islamist perspectives in a secular, multicultural environment. This public profile does not easily translate to Tripoli, Lebanon.

Bakri's intentions aside, I faced a decision regarding how to present my subject. Should I remain with the existing version of events or reflect the primary source's information? As a result, this book tells two stories: Bakri's version of his life is woven through the story of how Bakri was, *and allowed himself to be*, perceived. This is not, in any way, to suggest Bakri was a victim. The commonly-held version of his life, with its Muslim Brotherhood affiliations, expulsions and activism, is one that Bakri let stand in numerous interviews. I am not in a position to make absolute statements about whether it is Bakri's version or the media's version of history which is correct. In many ways, it is irrelevant and merely adds to the multilayered and complex currents which surround this field of inquiry.

This book, like most books on Islamism, probably raises more questions than it answers. It is a navigation of Islamic theory, multiculturalism, Islam in the West, media culture and Bakri's public profile. This book was intended to show the relationship between Islamism and its socio-political context. It suggests simple interpretations and binary stances cannot account for Islamism as a movement and, in particular, cannot account for Islamism in the West. It is my hope that these aims were achieved.

About the author

Kylie Baxter is a researcher and lecturer in the Centre for Muslim Minorities and Islam Policy Studies at Monash University. Her research interests include Muslim settlement in the West and Middle Eastern politics. She has published internationally on Islamism in the West and Middle Eastern politics. Her publications have appeared in the *Journal for Muslim Minority Affairs*, *Immigrants and Minorities* and *Middle East Policy*. She is also the author of *US Policy in the Middle East: the rise of anti-Americanism* (Routledge 2007).

Acknowledgments

This book was drawn from my PhD, which was completed at Monash University in 2007. I would like to extend my thanks to Associate Professor Shahram Akbarzadeh and my colleagues in the Centre for Muslim Minorities and Islam Policy Studies for their support and encouragement. Sincere thanks also to Emma Hegarty and Jenny Hall from the Monash Asia Institute for their tireless efforts with this manuscript. On a personal note, thanks to Kate, Scarlett, Eva and my family for their support during the researching of this book. This book was also greatly enhanced by conversations with Phil Rees and, in particular, Omar Bakri Muhammad Fostock, who was generous with his time in Tripoli, Lebanon in July 2007.

contents

	Preface	xi
	Glossary	xii
	Introduction	1
Part One	Muslims in the United Kingdom	9
Part Two	Contextualising Islamism	25
Part Three	Al-Muhajiroun	51
	Conclusion	89
	Bibliography	106

Preface

The present volume is the first in the 'Islam and Muslim Affairs Series'. This series is a collaborative endeavour between the Centre for Muslim Minorities and Islam Policy Studies and Monash University Press. This series offers a welcome opportunity for scholars to publish their research findings and bring their research activity to the attention of the community at large. The series is designed to contribute to the consolidation of the community of scholars on Islam and Muslim Affairs and to showcase Australian research excellence internationally.

This series consists of individual short books accessible to the academic community and the broader public through respected bookshops. The series is designed to disseminate research findings and contribute, in a measured and scholarly way, to contemporary public debate. All submitted manuscripts to this series are based on original research and are subjected to a double blind refereeing process.

Associate Professor Shahram Akbarzadeh
Series Editor

al-Muhajiroun	(the Emigrants), an organisation founded in Saudi Arabia and re-launched in the United Kingdom in the mid-1990s
as-salaf as-salih	the first generation of Muslims; the pious predecessors
a'qeedah	belief
da'wa	transmission of the faith; missionary movement
dar-al-Harb	the land of war; territories not governed by Islamic law
dar-al-Islam	the land of Islam (or peace); territory in which Islamic law prevails
fatwa	an Islamic legal ruling
hadith	a report of the saying or deeds of the Prophet as transmitted by his companions
hijra	the emigration of the Prophet from Mecca to Medina in 622
hizb al-Tahrir	The Liberation Party, founded in Palestine in the 1940s
kufr	(also kuffir, kufar, kufr/s) non-belief in God; the unbelievers
jahiliyya	the period of ignorance that existed in Arabia before the Islamic revelations
jihad	striving; an effort directed on behalf of the faith; physical and non-physical connotations
LAD	Local Authority District
MCB	Muslim Council of Britain
mujahideen	Muslim holy warriors

Qur'an	the Muslim scripture, the book containing the revelations of God to the Prophet Muhammad
revert	a person who has converted to Islam
shariah	the Muslim path (code, law, practice)
shia	a branch of Islam which views the Prophet's relative Ali and his heirs as the legitimate successors to the Prophet
sufi	a Muslim mystic, Islamic mysticism
sunna	the common practice of the Prophet and the early community which serves as an example to Muslims
sunni	Muslims who accept the legitimacy of the historical succession following the death of the Prophet
sura	a chapter of the Qur'an
takfir	the practice of declaring that an individual or a group previously considered Muslim is outside the faith (apostates)
tawhid	unity, the absolute oneness of God
UKACIA	UK Action Committee on Islamic Affairs
umma	the entire community of Muslim believers
watan	homeland

Introduction

Since the attacks in New York and Washington in 2001 and Madrid in 2003, authorities throughout the world have been warning of the inevitability of further terrorism against Western states. The London bombings of 7 July 2005 validated these concerns. Terrorist action, when it came to the United Kingdom, was perpetrated not by hardened al-Qaeda operatives but by young British Muslims. These men were inspired by Islamism, a political ideology which claims Islam as its nucleus. This movement has permeated all corners of the Muslim world and beyond. Islamism, despite its minority appeal in the Muslim world, has emerged as a significant challenge to the international community. The pervasive nature of the militant strand of Islamism has manifested in political violence against Western targets, especially since the launching of the US-led 'war on terror'. Rather than a centrally-directed organisation, international Islamism can be understood as a movement of loosely-affiliated individuals and organisations inspired by a set of central grievances and literalistic interpretations of specific Islamic doctrines. These core elements have inspired individuals and groups to undertake militant action in locations as diverse as Saudi Arabia, Madrid and Bali.

This movement has been strongly influenced by the work of numerous 18th and 19th century Muslim thinkers. However, modern Islamism is also a response to external factors. The movement that is today termed 'Islamism' emerged as a response to the political stagnation of Muslim societies in the early to mid-20th century. The movement was pioneered by individuals who were concerned by the Middle East's seeming inability to counter the physical presence and perhaps more importantly, the secularising influence of the West. The movement's radicalisation was a response to political catalysts such as the establishment of the state of Israel and the politically repressive environments fostered by mid-century secular-nationalist Arab regimes. Thus, Islamism is an indigenous response to internal change and external pressure. It is a product of modernity that draws on historic and theological traditions. Islamism was one way by which activists in the Middle East attempted to reform and re-shape their societies. Therefore, it is important to note that prior to the 1980s, the primary target of militant Islamists was not the 'West'; rather, it was local Arab/Muslim leaderships. While the intellectual roots of the movement are found in the early to mid-20th century, the focus of this study—contemporary militant Islamism, emerged during the period of the Cold War and the subsequent rise of the United States as the sole global power.

Islamism has proven to be a socio-political challenge throughout the Muslim world. In recent years, the movement has also constituted a challenge in many Western Muslim communities. In the United Kingdom the Islamist perspective is a minority viewpoint, condemned by the overwhelming majority of British Muslims. However, the terrorist attacks in Madrid and London signalled Islamism's violent emergence in Western multicultural state settings. The influence of Islamist doctrine on young Muslims in the West has confirmed the transferability of this worldview. The central question explored by this study is how did this movement, spawned in response to distinct social, political and religious experiences in the mid-20th century Middle East, carve a path into the contemporary United Kingdom?

As the attacks of 7 July 2005 demonstrated, Islamism found a receptive audience within a minority sub-set of the British Muslim community. Unfortunately, overwhelming condemnation of militant Islamism cannot always prevent the loss of life and damage that an isolated group of individuals can cause. The motivations and influences that encourage the few towards militancy are varied. Personal circumstances, beliefs, experiences, tensions in the process of migrant integration, socio-political marginalisation of Muslim minorities and the radicalising influence of the US-led 'war on terror' (often understood as a 'war on Islam') may all require exploration in this context. However, this study does not aim to account for the appeal of Islamism in the West; rather it is an exploration of how one organisation utilised the Islamist tradition to legitimise its perspective of the role of Muslims in the West.

Militant Islamism in the United Kingdom is perhaps suggestive of a phenomenon that could usefully be termed 'dual-incubation.' This term could be used to describe the process of radicalisation that appears to be affecting a tiny minority of Western Muslims. This term refers to two trends, or more specifically the collision of two trends, which influence young Western Muslims. These trends are the growing assertiveness and militancy of Islamism in Muslim-majority states and the challenges that remain present in the social, economic and political integration of young Muslims in Western states. Thus, the notion of 'dual incubation' refers to a double challenge: the appeal of militant Islamism with its focus on a sense of empowered and oppositional Islamic identity and the perceived failure of Western states to foster an inclusive sense of national belonging.

The young Western Muslims who are attracted to an Islamist worldview are representative of a new dimension of established international Islamism. The innovative nature of European Islamism is increasingly identified by scholars. As Paul Statham acknowledges, in Europe 'the revival of Islam has been as much if not more, a reaction to attempted integration processes, than a product of an alien culture imported by immigration' (Statham 2004:57). The acknowledgement that Islamism in Europe is affected simultaneously by the historical tradition of the Islamist movement and the reality of the Muslim minority experience suggests the question: to what extent do Western Islamist organisations fit within the established paradigm of Islamism, a movement nurtured within the context of the Muslim world? This question holds serious implications for how Western states, Western Muslim communities and national societies understand and respond to the challenge of Islamism in the West. It also indicates the need for the development of new analysis and interpretation, a process to which this study offers a contribution.

Militant Islamism, as evident in the failed attacks of late June 2007, continues to present a significant threat to national security in the West. Historically speaking, the dissemination of Islamism in the West was often initiated by Arab preachers. However, Islamism appears to have struck a chord within small sections of the second and third generation British Muslim community, a significant proportion of which is of South Asian descent. This is an interesting development as, while the South Asian region has produced several important Islamist thinkers, the movement has been predominately associated with the Arab world.

The willingness of young British-born Muslims to engage in acts of terrorism is a deeply concerning precedent for all Western Muslim communities. However, this debate needs to be kept in perspective. As the United Kingdom Home Office has pointed out, 'the number of British Muslims actively engaged in terrorist activity, whether at home or abroad, or supporting such activity, is extremely small and estimated at less than 1%' (UKFCO 2004). The inspiration for such actions may well be Islamism, yet this study argues that the catalyst for militancy may be more closely linked to the failing or perceived failing of the existing national system. Thus Western Islamism, a movement still in its infancy, may require different academic and practical approaches to those applied in the Muslim world. Western Islamist groups draw on the same tenets that sustain their brother organisations in the Middle East, but the trigger for radicalisation may be more firmly rooted in a mixture of warped theology, the experience of minority status, the perceived failings of Western states to offer an inclusive and equitable identity structure for all citizens and residents, and an internalisation of global political crises.

The catalyst for militancy aside, the media and public focus on 'British Muslim terrorists' performs the function of driving a wedge between the mainstream British Muslim community, which is deeply opposed to terrorist action in the name of 'Islam', and the broader British society. This in turn fosters an environment of suspicion and intolerance that only feeds the sense of sociopolitical alienation that may be central to the appeal of Islamism in the West. Moreover, the challenge presented by this movement is intensified by its fluid and adaptive nature. Theological or intellectual attempts to combat Islamism struggle as the ill-defined political agenda of Western Islamism lends itself to the view that the movement is predominately an expression of criminality, in which violence has become the end product. This violence is shrouded in the language of traditional Islamism to lend it a sense of legitimacy and purpose. Islamists in the Muslim world have some chance of achieving political change by either militant means or through popular change. In the West, the Islamist political agenda, usually expressed through a desire for a Sharia-based society, holds little relevance. In order to contextualise these arguments, this study provides insights into the experience of British Muslims in the 20th century and compares the theological and intellectual tenets of historic Islamism to the agenda of one contemporary British Islamist organisation.

The organisation under investigation here is the now-defunct al-Muhajiroun. Al-Muhajiroun was a fringe minority organisation that operated in London from the mid-1990s to 2004. Sheikh Omar Bakri Muhammad[1] established a group of students as an offshoot of the global Hizb al-Tahrir in Saudi Arabia in 1983. As a result of his migration to the United Kingdom in the mid-1990s, Bakri re-launched his organisation, al-Muhajiroun. The mainstream British Muslim community overwhelmingly rejected al-Muhajiroun and its divisive platform. As the 'war on terror' gained pace, al-Muhajiroun's rhetoric responded. The organisation was adept at securing media attention and the sensationalist nature of Britain's tabloids greatly assisted the group's leaders. By the time of its closure in 2004, the organisation was reported as calling for Muslims to engage in acts of violence against the state. In stark contrast to the perspective of many British Muslim organisations, al-Muhajiroun's worldview was underpinned by a belief in the supposed incompatibility of Islamic and Western norms. The group focused on the need for a militant interpretation of jihad and strongly rejected the concept of loyalty to the secular state. It used these two themes as its major publicity and recruitment levers. In this way, through its blending of a key element of historical Islamism and the reality of the responsibilities and expectations in the modern West, al-Muhajiroun constituted a strong example of the notion of 'dual-incubation.'

This study provides insight into how an organisation that was drawn from, and functioned in, a multicultural Western state understood itself as part of a tradition indigenous to the Muslim world. Through the exploration of Islamic concepts such as jihad, this study seeks to explore the nexus between Islamic history and contemporary British politics. This book is not an exploration of why individual Muslims would join an organisation such as al-Muhajiroun. In the excellent *Radical Islam Rising: Islamic Extremism in the West*, Quintain Wiktorowicz has provided a detailed account of what encourages people to embrace what he terms 'high-risk activism' (Wiktorowicz 2005). Wiktorowicz asserts that al-Muhajiroun appealed predominately to young religious-seekers. Generally, the organisation's recruits had a poor understanding of Islam, a dissatisfaction with the often culturally influenced religious tradition offered by the older generation and a sense of alienation from the British societal system of which they were meant to be a part (Wiktorowicz 2007:107). Al-Muhajiroun, and the charismatic Sheikh at its helm, capitalised upon this sense of dislocation through a highly-organised process of indoctrination and activism. It focused on the local challenges facing Muslims in the United Kingdom and linked them to broader, and timely, issues such as the fate of Palestine, Afghanistan and Iraq. In this way, al-Muhajiroun presented a highly politicised version of 'Islamic identity' to generate a climate of inclusiveness and support for its followers. As the British media and the mainstream Muslim community stepped up its condemnation, the organisation's defiant siege mentality intensified. The current study seeks to situate al-Muhajiroun's practice and theory within the broader context of British Muslim history and international Islamism. This book also picks up where Wiktorowicz's 2004 study concludes, charting the organisation's downfall and Bakri's departure from the United Kingdom in mid-2005.

This study is divided into three major sections. Part One offers a brief statistical and historical overview of Muslims in Britain, with a focus on moments of politicisation such as the Rushdie Affair of 1989. Part Two explores elements of the Islamist tradition. Given the overall focus on al-Muhajiroun, this section explores Islamism through the experience of al-Muhajiroun's parent organisation, Hizb al-Tahrir. It also studies the pivotal notion of jihad, especially in the thought of the Muslim Brotherhood's Sayyid Qutb. It is from these two currents: the history of British Muslims and the Islamist movement with its focus on the notion of militant jihad that the organisation al-Muhajiroun emerged. In Part Three, al-Muhajiroun is situated within the Islamist paradigm. This is achieved by tracing the development of the al-Muhajiroun organisation in Saudi Arabia in the mid-1980s and its eventual emergence in London in the mid-1990s. Finally, this study touches upon the other major proponents of Islamism in the United Kingdom in this period before assessing the downfall of al-Muhajiroun and its legacy.

The underlying area of inquiry here is the field of Western Islam. In particular, this is a study of the various responses of British Muslims and, more broadly, British society to an Islamist organisation operating in a period in part defined by Western military action in the Muslim world. Al-Muhajiroun is by no means representative. The Islamist worldview the organisation propagated constitutes a marginal response to the question of Islamic identity, either in the West or in the Muslim world. Al-Muhajiroun, which claimed an international presence, operated predominately in the United Kingdom and it is within the context of the British state that the organisation is explored. Al-Muhajiroun categorically rejected Western norms such as democracy, multiculturalism and secularism. However, the organisation was, simultaneously, part of a Western society. This study explores the political, ideological and religious traditions that al-Muhajiroun utilised in its attempt to legitimise its presence in and rejection of the West.

Al-Muhajiroun's lifespan in Britain covered the mid-1990s to 2004. The organisation could only ever claim a marginal minority membership. Yet its message was widely disseminated by both the organisation itself and by the tabloid media willing to feed it the oxygen of publicity it needed to survive. Thus, this study strongly focuses on the role of the media and public perceptions of the Islamist agenda. Considering its emergence from the international Hizb al-Tahrir, and its collapse into a series of smaller splinter organisations, al-Muhajiroun can be seen as a brief episode in the on-going evolution of international, and more specifically Western, Islamism.

Notes

1. Bakri's full name is Omar Bakri Muhammad Fostock. In this book he is referred to as Bakri, in line with most media sources.

part one

Muslims in the United Kingdom

A contemporary statistical overview

The demographics of Muslim communities have been the focus of government and public scrutiny in recent years. In Britain, the overall economic status of the Muslim community is a source of enduring concern. As Dr Abdul Bari, Secretary General of the Muslim Council of Britain (MCB) has been keen to point out, there exists great socio-economic diversity within the Muslim community. Sub-sections of the community, such as Asian-African Muslims, many of whom immigrated to the United Kingdom with higher levels of education, have markedly different experiences (Cook 2006). However, various economic quality of life indicators reveal that British Muslims, particularly the Pakistani and to an even greater level the Bangladeshi communities, are amongst the most deprived sections of British society. The Muslim community of Britain constitutes 22.8% of Britain's total minority ethnic population (White 2002:5). In the early years of the 21st century, estimates of the number of Muslims residing in Britain ranged from 1.6 million (ONS 2001g) to 1.8 million (*Guardian* 2002). Thus, Muslims constitute roughly 3% of the total British population. All sources concur that Muslims are the second largest faith group in the United Kingdom.

The Muslim community is ethnically diverse, including people of Arabic, Turkish, Persian, East European and African backgrounds. However, as roughly half the community share South Asian ancestry, it is this ethnic and cultural tradition that often frames the British Muslim community. The influence of South Asian norms is further reinforced by the ethnically and culturally fragmented composition of the remainder of the community. As with any categorisation, the term 'South Asian' should be used with caution, as it spans numerous and often overlapping identities. The term refers to a diverse community group that includes people of differing socio-economic standing, various national backgrounds (including those of Indian, Sri Lankan, Bangladeshi and Pakistani descent) and numerous religious affiliations (Hindu, Sikh and Muslim). In this context, the focus is upon the Pakistani and Bangladeshi communities, which are overwhelmingly Muslim. While a range of socio-economic experiences exist even within these communities, statistical data suggests these two national sub-sets are among Britain's most economically and socially disadvantaged minority groupings.

In accordance with established minority settlement patterns, Muslims tend to cluster together, with 38% of the total community residing in the London area (ONS 2001d). While Muslims only constitute 8% of London's population overall, there are certain districts where the concentration is much higher. For example, Muslims constitute 36% of the population of the Local Authority District (LADs) of Tower Hamlets and 24% of the district of Newham (ONS 2001d). Both these LADs are economically deprived. This reflects broader trends. In 2000, Muslims were over-represented in the LADs that were deprived.[1] This residential pattern has implications for socio-political integration as well as the obvious economic concerns.

As stated, a significant proportion of the Muslim community is of South Asian descent (43% Pakistani and 16% Bangladeshi) (ONS 2001c). In 2001 a small proportion of the community (4%) were reverts,[2] meaning Muslims from a 'white British' background (ONS 2001c). Just under half (46%) of Muslims living in Great Britain in 2001 had been born locally (ONS 2001b). Furthermore, in 2004, 70% of Muslims gave their national identity as British (ONS 2001b). This result interplays with other attitudinal data findings, such as the 2004 survey commissioned by the Islamic Human Rights Commission, that found 40% of 1125 respondents reported a sense or very strong sense of belonging to Britain (Ameli & Merali 2004:42). While changes in socio-political climate may play a part, the difficulty of citing attitudinal data is underscored by results in the 2000–02 periods, in which much higher positive responses to similar questions of loyalty/affiliation were obtained (UKFCO 2004).

Formal statistical data provides a clearer insight into community structure. The British Muslim community is predominately young. This reflects global trends in Muslim communities. In Great Britain, Muslims have the youngest age profile of all religious groups. In 2001, 34% of Muslims were under the age of 16 (ONS 2001a). This can be further broken down by ethnic groupings, with 34% of Pakistani Muslims and 40% of Bangladeshi Muslims under 15 years of age (ONS 2001h). These figures are significant when juxtaposed against the national average where only 20.2% of the population is younger than 15 years of age. In a linked statistic, Muslim families are also generally larger than non-Muslim families. The indication is that this will remain the case, as the average intended number of children among Pakistani and Bangladeshi women was 3.4 and 3.6 respectively, compared with 2.4 among Indian women and 2.1 among white women (ONS 2001f).

This young, rapidly expanding community is playing an increasing role in British public and political consciousness. This suggests a promising future. However, overall the British Muslim community also emerges as disadvantaged in an analysis of educational indicators. These trends are more noticeable within the Pakistani and Bangladeshi communities than amongst Muslims from other backgrounds. The higher education rate for Pakistanis is 49% and for Bangladeshis 39%; this is on par with or higher than the participation rate for the non-Muslim community, which stands at 38% (DWP 2005). However, as is the case in most transgenerational migrant communities, this is not replicated across the entire age-span of the community. For example, Pakistanis and Bangladeshis are also the ethnic groups most likely to be unqualified, as 48% of Bangladeshi women, 40% of Bangladeshi men, and 40% of Pakistani women and 27% of Pakistani men have no qualification (White 2002:12).

These high rates of youth participation in tertiary education should translate into a significant and growing presence in the skilled workforce. However, in 2005 the Minister for Employment, Margaret Hodge, revealed that only 76% of Muslim graduates of working age were in skilled jobs, compared with the overall graduate rate of 87%. This translates into an 11% gap (DWP 2005) and can perhaps be attributed in part to workplace discrimination, which the Muslim community reported has increased in the past five years. A Home Office report published in 2001 recorded these trends:

> a consistently higher level of unfair treatment was reported by Muslim organisations than by most other religious groups; unfair treatment in every aspect of education, employment, housing, law and order, and in all the local government services (Weller, Feldman & Pudman 2001:vii).

Unemployment figures for the Muslim community rose dramatically outside the graduate cohort. In employment statistics, the Bangladeshi community fared worse than any other ethnic group. Over 40% of young Bangladeshi males were unemployed in 2001; in the same cohort for white men the figure was 12% (White 2002:9). In 2004, Muslims had the highest male unemployment rate in Great Britain, at 13% (ONS 2004a). The national average in the same period was 4.8%, a thirty-year low. Breaking the figure down by religious groupings, Muslims aged 25 and over were more than three times as likely as Christians of the same age to be unemployed, a figure of 11% and 3% respectively (ONS 2004a). These labour market realities contributed to a situation where social security benefits constituted 19% of Pakistani and Bangladeshi household income.[3]

As mentioned, statistics reveal the community's educational profile is changing. UK-born Muslims were more likely than those born elsewhere to have a degree or equivalent qualification (ONS 2004b). However, recent surveys suggest that even for this cohort discrimination will be an obstacle. The Islamic Human Rights Commission report that of a sample of 1125 respondents, 85% of employed Muslims reported subjective discrimination in the workplace (Ameli, Manzur and Merali 2004). This, mixed with cultural norms and a lack of employment opportunities, has perhaps contributed to a higher inclination towards self-employment. Pakistani men in particular demonstrate a strong tendency to be self-employed (within sectors such as transport, communication and hospitality).[4]

In addition to the data on education and employment, Muslim males and females in Great Britain had the highest rates of reported ill health in 2001 (ONS 2001e). This was greater in the older age groups with Bangladeshis most likely to report ill health in their 40s and 50s (48%), compared with only 10% of white adults in the same age bracket (NHSHDA 2001). These figures reflect recent trends, as in 1999 Bangladeshis and Pakistanis were three to four times more likely to rate their health as bad or very bad. More specifically, Bangladeshis were over six times more likely to have diabetes than the general population (White 2002:14).

Even prior to the events of 11 September 2001, and the current climate of tension generated by the 'war on terror' and the increase in international and domestic terrorism, British Muslims were more likely to suffer racially-based attacks than any other group. Considering the politics of fear often generated about Western Muslim communities this fact is particularly important. In 1999, Pakistanis and Bangladeshis faced a risk ratio of 4.2%, while the risk of suffering racially-motivated violence for a non-Muslim stood at 0.3%.[5] In a 2001 survey, the majority of Muslim respondents thought 'hostility, abuse and unfair media coverage had become more frequent' over the preceding five years (Weller, Feldman & Pudman 2001:vii). In the context of the 'war on terror' and especially after the 7 July 2005 terrorist attacks in London, the statistics on racially-motivated or faith-related discrimination and violence soared.

The question of socio-political parity is also important. The pressure upon Muslims to justify or adapt their cultural and religious practices to reflect mainstream norms is significant. However, the state often makes little attempt at reciprocal adaptation. The area of primary education is central to this tension. State-maintained faith-based schools have proven a battle ground between minorities and the state for two generations. Traditionally, the state has maintained a range of Christian, predominately Church of England, schools. In 2001, 5.1 million children aged five to 16 in England were described as Christian, with state-maintained Christian schools offering 1.7 million places. In other words, 33.3% of Christian children have the opportunity to receive a faith-based education (DES 2004).

It is not surprising that these statistics are not uniformly carried over into minority communities. However, within the three minority communities of Jews, Sikhs and Muslims, significant differences are evident. The more established Jewish community has been the most successful minority in this regard with 33,000 Jewish school-aged children in England serviced by 13,000 places in state-maintained Jewish schools, a situation that allows 39.3% of Jewish children to attend a Jewish school (DES 2004). The ratio for Muslim and Sikh children to school places has been much lower. There were 371,000 school-aged Muslim children in England in 2001 and 1,100 places in four Muslim state-maintained schools in 2004 (DES 2004). This provides the Muslim community with an extremely limited opportunity to enrol their children in a Muslim school. The statistics are similar for the Sikh community, with 64,000 school-aged children and only two schools with a total of 600 places (DES 2004).

The statistical data on the British Muslim community suggests two important themes. First, as a community, British Muslims, particularly those of Pakistani and Bangladeshi origin, are among the most disadvantaged sections of British society. Second, the British Muslim community is overwhelmingly young, and rapidly expanding. The educational indicators demonstrate the community is steadily progressing. However, assessing the statistics as a whole, it can be suggested that without meaningful change in the communal economic, educational and socio-political fortunes of some sections, the pressure on the wider Muslim community of which they are a significant part will only intensify. The contemporary economic indicators tell only a small part of the British Muslim story. The responses of the state, the broader community and the impact of historical and political events have also shaped the experiences of Muslims in Britain. These historical experiences proved vital to the politicisation of the community and the development of an engaged public presence.

Muslims in the United Kingdom: the historical experience

To further contextualise the emergence of Islamism in the United Kingdom, a brief historical exploration of Muslim settlement and the community's legal status, politicisation and interaction with the mainstream British society is required.[6] The British Muslim community is marked by specific cultural, legal and political experiences in late 20th century Britain. The emergence of an Islamist perspective is only one element of a thriving, diverse community that houses a diversity of views. The ability of the mainstream Muslim community to effectively and publicly counter manifestations of Islamism in Britain speaks also of a community increasingly assured in the public domain of a multicultural political discourse.

The United Kingdom's initial major Muslim settlement began in the mid-20th century. The first settler community was comprised of economic migrants, men from throughout the British Empire seeking employment in post-war Britain (Joly 1988:33). The concentration of South Asian men in the working class areas of London and other regional centres signalled a new phase in the construction of a multi-ethnic 'British' identity. The legal status of these men was unambiguous; as colonial subjects helping to rebuild the war-torn motherland, they were immediately afforded full British citizenship. This reflected the legal norms enshrined in the *British Nationality and Aliens Act* of 1914 that, as a legislative legacy of Imperial Britain, focused on the notion of Empire and loyalty to the Crown. Thus, until 1962 individuals born throughout the Empire held the status of British subject and upon arrival in the United Kingdom were offered full citizenship. Many of these men viewed their position in the United Kingdom as an economically driven, temporary arrangement. While formally protected as citizens of the state, these early Muslim settlers maintained distinct ethnic and cultural identities. These simultaneously-held identities tested popular notions of belonging that tended to blur the legal status of citizenship and a social or cultural sense of 'Britishness'.

As the 1960s and 1970s progressed, the early settlers became increasingly entrenched. This trend was solidified by the arrival of wives and children (Joly 1988:33; Vertovec 2002:19). The *Commonwealth Immigration Act* was passed in 1962 in response to the rapid development of distinct communities. This Act limited immigration previously aimed at fulfilling unskilled labour needs. Further restrictions on immigration were then passed in 1968, 1969, 1971 and 1981 (Vertovec 1996:173). Nonneman and others have argued that periods of economic hardship often reveal fissures between settler and host communities; this supposition was validated by a downturn in relations between Muslims and the mainstream in certain regions through the 1970s (Nonneman 1996:16).

Despite these challenges, the Muslim communities of Britain developed quickly. Continued restrictions to immigration law encouraged individuals to utilise legal provisions for family reunification, a trend that saw the local replication of tribal and clan- based affiliations from South Asia. Even though tentative attempts at community-based political organisation were made, the community as a whole remained relatively apolitical. This is not to suggest the level of integration into British politics was high. The British system has been described as one of 'civic pluralism', whereby access to the political community of the state is assured for migrants, however, it is not 'conditional upon assimilation and [minorities] are allowed to retain their cultural identities' (Koopmans & Statham 2003:209). Yet this pluralist ideal was challenged by other, more exclusionary, trends within the British socio-political mindset. As

Caryl Phillips has pointed out, 'Britain has always sought to define her people and by extension the nation by identifying those who don't belong' (Phillips 1997:x). These two approaches: civic pluralism and exclusionary national identity are clearly contradictory.

On a societal level, Britain's organising political principle is multiculturalism, a doctrine that literally affirms the presence of a multitude of cultures. However, the premise of British *multi*culturalism has been understood as a plurality of *racial* groups living together. Thus, the emergence of a Muslim community that increasingly identified as a faith-based group provided a significant challenge to the multicultural status quo. Modood (2005:206) outlines the impact of this development, suggesting 'the emergence of Muslim political agency has thrown British multiculturalism into theoretical and practical disarray'.

In the mid to late 1970s the British Muslim community had become increasingly politically active. As part of this process, many British Muslims agitated for a full recognition of their individual and communal socio-political rights. As part of the institutionalisation of multiculturalism in the United Kingdom, the *Race Relations Act* of 1976 recognised Jews and Sikhs as distinct communities. However, the Muslim community was not recognised in the same fashion. This reflected a political approach to multiculturalism that was based on ethnicity and was influenced by the historic American model. However, in defence of the British approach in this period, it should be acknowledged that the development and implementation of Race Relations legislation did in itself constitute recognition that 'that political equality [had] not led to equal treatment' (Koopmans & Statham 2003:209–10). Intentions aside, the outcome of this legislation was that Muslims continued to be recognised only within the paradigm of their ethnicity. Retrospectively, this legislation can be understood as a point of political awakening for British Muslims as the question of exactly what role religion played in identity formulation was brought firmly into the open.

The ethnic, as opposed to religious, focus of the British approach to multiculturalism has been increasingly challenged by Muslim scholars. As Modood (2003:110) explains, 'Muslim identity is seen as the illegitimate child of British multiculturalism'. Indeed, in a state where 'racial categories form the cornerstone of race relations and equal opportunities policies,' (Koopmans & Statham 2003:217) the socio-political willingness to accept religion as the basis of a communal identity has proven limited. As mentioned, a legacy of the colonial period was that early Muslim settlers and thus their families were predominately assured of the legal security offered by citizenship. This individual protection under the law led to a flourishing community increasingly active in the public sphere and willing to challenge the prevailing conceptions of religion and its place in a multicultural, predominately secular, state. Since the 1970s, a diversity of political and social organisations has been a feature of the British Muslim community. These organisations span the spectrum of religiousity and advocate for a broad range of social and political causes. In the first years of the 21st century, the proportion of British Muslims holding citizenship was placed at approximately 93% (An-Na'im 2006:38). The security of citizenship may well have empowered British Muslims to organise politically to a level rarely matched in other European Union countries.

Religious affiliations of British Muslims

The role of religion in the identity formation of individuals and the community became increasingly prominent during the 1980s. The British Muslim community, while slightly diversified as a result of African and Arab immigration in the late 1970s, remained predominately of South Asian descent. The religious affiliations in the British Muslim community therefore generally reflected those of Pakistan and Bangladesh. The majority of British Muslims are Sunni Muslims, mostly adherents of the Hanafi school. In Britain, religious and cultural movements emerged that were often transposed from and affiliated to organisations in the subcontinent. The two dominant South Asian religious groups in the United Kingdom have been, and remain, the Deobandi and Barelvi streams of Islam.

John Rex, a researcher on religious affiliation in the British Muslim community, asserted that the Barelvi stream is the largest within the South Asian Muslim community (Rex 2002:59). This is supported by James Piscatori who credited the stream with retaining the adherence of 60% of the United Kingdom's Muslim community (Piscatori 1990:786). This stream of Islam is traditionalist, especially in relation to social teachings (Rex 1996:221). However, the Sufi influence is also evident as adherents believe in the power of intercession, undertaken by religious figures known as *pirs*, who disseminate a 'custom laden version of Islam' that has clear roots in the subcontinent experience (Geaves 1999:366). The Deobandi stream, in contrast, often rejects Sufism as un-Islamic. This stream emphasises a literalistic scriptural approach to Islam (Piscatori 1990:786). Despite its weaker numerical strength, Rex has suggested that the Deobandi stream has at times exercised considerable influence through its disproportionate control of mosques (Rex 2002:58). While these two streams hold significant differences, especially in relation to the influence and legitimacy of Sufi teachings on Islam, they have co-existed successfully in the United Kingdom.

The transnational nature of Islam places the British Muslim community in an unusual position in comparison to other minority groups. For example, funding has been sought and obtained from external sources (Rex 1996:232). Throughout the 1980s, Iran and Saudi Arabia tussled for religious and ideological leadership of the Muslim world. The two states sought to fulfil expansive visions. Iran, still guided by Khomeini, engaged in the attempt to 'export the revolution', while proponents of Saudi Arabia's Wahhabi doctrine also sought international influence. Attracting Muslims to their respective doctrines became an objective both states pursued throughout the Muslim world and beyond. In Britain, the aims of external actors were perhaps aided by the withdrawal of state-funding from community groups under the Thatcher Government, a situation that caused many to dissolve. The organisational void within the Muslim community thus offered an open field to religious groups, both domestic and international. The Iranian/Saudi influence manifested itself primarily in the funding and support of various Islamic institutions that, in turn, propagated a particular viewpoint. While this tension and the various British Muslim organisations that attempted to exploit it affected the politicisation of Islam within the United Kingdom, caution is required in placing too strong an emphasis on the influence of external state actors upon the British Muslim community. For example, in a situation explored by Nielsen (2005), when faced with perceived Iraqi aggression in 1991, the Saudi government sought to 'call in the chips' and gain statements of support from its allied sections in the British Muslim community. However, as Pnina Werbner (1996:115) demonstrated, this attempt failed. The Saudi-backed mosques limited themselves to statements of condemnation regarding the Western invasion of Iraq, and avoided commenting on the fate of the widely unpopular al-Saud regime.

The linking of British Muslims to events in the Muslim world predates the events of 1991. A series of politically-charged events had occurred that transformed the British Muslim community. These developments led to an increasing identification of a disjuncture between the legal rights and the socio-political realities of citizenship. The social discourse of multiculturalism in some ways assumes that the 'cultures' it brings together are distinct, unified entities. Thus, multiculturalism had fostered an approach that, although allowing for the diversity of British society, often obscured the multiplicity of perspectives within the Muslim community itself. Within the emergent 'them and us' paradigm, Muslim attempts at political organisation were often misunderstood as a reflection of unity rather than diversity. Concurrently, multiculturalism was often popularly understood not as plurality of cultures co-existing, but rather as the willingness of Anglo-Saxon England *to accept* the presence of other cultures.

This was reinforced by media coverage that represented the Muslim community as a united, often threatening, presence within the United Kingdom. It was further underscored by the application of British law. As discussed, Muslims in Britain predominately hold citizenship status; however, Muslims were not offered legal protection as a minority community. Furthermore, blasphemy laws were not extended to cover the denigration of Islam. This unequal status of religion, and by extension identity, was brought to the forefront of British politics in the 1980s.

Decisive moments such as the establishment of Dr Kalim Siddiqui's Iranian-backed Muslim Institute, the Honeyford affair,[7] the battle over the provision of halal meats in schools and, most infamously the Rushdie affair of 1989, thrust a generation of Muslims into the media and public spotlight. According to Nielsen, by the late 1980s the Muslim community was characterised by two distinguishing features, 'the comparative legal security of citizenship or the residential status of commonwealth citizens and the relatively lengthy period that the major proportion had lived [in the UK]' (Nielsen 1988:54). However, as Nielsen also points out, the other resounding norm within the community was the increasing belief that citizenship and multiculturalism with their 'alleged equal status, were in practice more imagined than real' (Nielsen 1988:161). The tension between the Muslim community's understandings of its own legal and social legitimacy and the failure of the dominant culture to fulfil the promised rights increased. The Rushdie affair of 1989, with its combination of literary achievement, freedom of speech, hysterical media reactions and the issuing of the Iranian fatwa, emerged as the pivotal moment for a new generation of Muslims.

The 1988 publication of Salman Rushdie's novel *The Satanic Verses*, sparked a controversy that engulfed the British Muslim community. While presented as a novel, the Rushdie text contained negative portrayals of characters clearly based on the personage of the Prophet Muhammad and his wives. Denigration of Islamic figures was not a new phenomenon in Western literary circles; however, the obvious difference in this case was the identity of the text's author, Salman Rushdie. While Rushdie did not identify himself as a Muslim, he was born into a Muslim family of Pakistani origins.

In the initial phase following the text's publication, the Rushdie affair was largely an internal debate that divided the community. Initially the response to the text demonstrated the determination to defend the faith from attack and revealed concerns over the changing nature of religious identity. These issues manifested in a power struggle between generations, and between radical and moderate community elements. However, as community anger intensified, some within the British Muslim community petitioned the publishers, Penguin, to withdraw the book, a request that was declined. The UK Action Committee on Islamic Affairs (UKACIA) then agitated for the application of the blasphemous libel law to prosecute the book's publishers and to prevent distribution.

The UKACIA took the case to the House of Lords, which upheld a 1977 decision that the blasphemous libel law could not be extended beyond Christianity. The legal battle was finally resolved in the High Court, where the inapplicability of the blasphemy laws to Islam was once again reaffirmed. The British legal system's refusal to apply to Islam the same protection which was afforded to Christianity raised the question of parity, which in turn underscored differences in legal (and social and political) treatment of Muslim concerns. The international ramifications of this situation became evident on 14 February 1989, when Iran's Ayatollah Khomeini issued a fatwa proclaiming a death sentence upon Salman Rushdie and 'all those involved in the publication of the book who were aware of its content'.[8]

Interpretations of the Rushdie affair are diverse. However, at a base level the primary theme that emerged was the Muslim determination to be accorded socio-political parity. The public backlash revealed much about the tensions inherent within multiculturalism in the British state. Muslims, while far from united on the Rushdie text, and even more disunited in their views of the controversy that surrounded it, generally shared a fundamental concern over the denigration of the Prophet and the seeming inability of British society to respect their faith (McGown 1999:174). Within the British media, the 1989 book burning by a small group of Muslims and the response of the Iranian clerics, was often falsely presented as a unified, or majority, perspective. This approach both stigmatised Muslims and submerged the many real differences and nuances in the British Muslim response. The focus on the Iranian fatwa in particular served to present Muslims as holding fundamentally different values from that of the mainstream. The difficulties the Muslim community faced in transmitting its discontent with the legal and public handling of the Rushdie affair encouraged many Muslims to consider the community's access to power and its public presence.

The Rushdie affair propelled questions regarding the place of Islam in Britain into the public arena. Internally, the saga highlighted questions of authority, public presence, intercultural relations, generational differences and the role of international Islamic players. It also revealed that defence of the faith and the central personage of the Prophet Muhammad had the ability to transcend sectarian differences in the Muslim community (McGown 1999:174). While the Iranian fatwa was generally unpopular, it did serve to link British Muslims with the 'ultimate symbol of Islamic revival,' the Islamic Republic of Iran

(Zubaida 1998:89). This raised important questions regarding the intensity of transnational identification and encouraged many Muslims to consider the nexus between Islam, Britain and the Muslim world. To organisations such as Siddiqui's Iranian-backed Muslim Institute, the Rushdie affair demonstrated the power of Islam both globally and locally (Siddiqui 1990:7). However, in contrast to the Iranian position, the Saudi Arabian-backed clerics and institutions in the United Kingdom did not express support for the fatwa (Piscatori 1990:782). These divergent views reflected the ideological struggle between Saudi Arabi and Iran in this period and their search for influence within the British Muslim community.

The involvement of Khomeini's regime, while publicly premised on a defence of Islam, only served the interests of those factions seeking to marginalise Muslims in Britain. The fatwa was a theocratic response to an issue that spoke more intensely of domestic politics and identity formulation in Britain. While the Rushdie text clearly and undoubtedly distressed, dismayed and angered many Muslims, the controversy it sparked was also related to the lack of intercultural discourse and respect in Britain. The co-existence element of institutionalised multiculturalism was tested in the call for mutual respect and protection of religious identity, and it largely failed. Thus, the Rushdie affair entrenched the determination of the British Muslim community to pursue its 'claim to rights' theoretically enshrined within the multicultural paradigm of the British state (Koopmans & Statham 2003:199). The major legacy of the Rushdie Affair was therefore an increased awareness of the need for a new generation of individuals who could meaningfully express Muslim concerns within the mainstream.

British Muslims and transnational Islam

These two levels of analysis, the socio-economic standing and the socio-political history of the community, provide important background context for the following exploration of Islamism in Britain. The statistical data explored above provides an insight into the socio-economic situation of Muslims in Britain. Statistical information necessitates the drawing of generalised conclusions regarding the overall status of a community. Reviewing the data, any notion of a link between extremism and poverty is tenuous at best. Indeed, surveying the statistical information available it appears nonsensical. A correlation between economic disadvantage and extremism would, particularly among Muslims of Pakistani and South Asian descent, see a much greater extremist impulse.

The socio-political history of Muslim settlement in Britain reveals the existence of a community that is well-established and engaged in the public discourses of the state. As the community developed, communal identity structures also emerged. The order of terms in the designation of 'British' Muslims is revealing. It presupposes two distinct identities—'British' and 'Muslim'—and suggests that a sense of 'Britishness' is the first and foremost marker of identity. However, the notion of Britishness as the normative marker of identity has been, for some, challenged by the concurrent Islamic sense of self. This potential theoretical and practical tension emerges more forcefully in moments of external or situational pressure, moments where some Muslims feel they face stark choices between loyalty to the British state and membership of a transnational religious group. The British Muslim community has historically experienced such moments, based on both domestic and international factors, and these developments have engendered diverse responses. An increased awareness of the need for intercultural dialogue has been the dominant response. However, a rejection of the status quo and the methodology (both social and political) with which the state and British society has engaged with the Muslim community has been another reaction.

The increasing role of Islam as a marker of identity is a sub-theme to this historical period. However, the embrace of Islam in the context of identity construction in the West required significant adaptation and flexibility. From a textual position, Islam could offer little guidance on appropriate organisational principles for Muslims living as a religious minority in a society governed by un-Islamic normative values such as secularism. The Qur'an and the classical Islamic tradition simply presupposed Muslims were the majority in their society. The dearth of textual guidance for modern Muslims living outside the Muslim world has been noted by many scholars. Moreover, among others, Werbner has recognised the lack of jurisprudential precedent for voluntary migration, which is modern history's norm (2000: 113). In 1991, Jorgen Nielsen (1991:49) cautioned that Muslims in Europe were often perceived by the broader community not according to their own actions but through the prism of international events such as the Iranian Revolution and the Lebanese civil war. This observation remains relevant. Contemporary European society is inundated with images of the 'war on terror', which is directed against Muslim-majority states and organisations. The coverage of bloodshed and violence between Muslims, and also between Muslims and non-Muslim armies in the Middle East is continual. The subsequent, nearly generic casting of Muslims in an oppositional role clearly influences the relationship between Western Muslim minorities and the broader societies of which they are part.

The emphasis placed on the Islamic aspects of identity is a matter of individual choice, and is influenced by a range of factors including familial tradition, generational norms and personal experiences. Jocelyne Cesari (2003:253) notes that 'sectarian, ethnic and nationalist groupings, in many cases, play a more prominent role in Muslim identity than any abstract notion of a universal brotherhood of believers'. Cesari is right to underscore the abstract nature of the concept of the *umma*. However, as Roy (2005:361) suggests, for Islamists the notion of the *umma* has proven a potent 'abstract universal'. Following this line of thought, it is the contention here that the notion of the *umma* has become an increasingly important influence on identity formation in sections of the British Muslim community. Naturally, transnational identification does not imply an embrace of an Islamist worldview. Indeed, many activists and organisations which advocate for Muslim interests internationally explicitly condemn Islamism. However, the notion of the *umma* and the sense of shared community and belonging it can provide are relevant to understanding the appeal of Islamism in the West. This is particularly the case when alternative structures of belonging, such as the national community, are seen as lacking or exclusionary.

It is precisely the abstraction of the notion of the *umma* that is seized upon by Islamists as they attempt to forge an alternate identity structure for the disaffected young Muslims who constitute their target audience. The appeal of this concept is self-evident. In Islamic history the *umma* is, put simply, the idea that 'Muslims all over the world are brothers and sisters despite their history, region, culture, colour, language, or socio-economic and political status' (Husain 1997:107). The lack of textual precedent for Muslim minorities has been noted. Yet the Islamic jurisprudential tradition does engage with the notion of Muslim life in non-Muslim states, largely by affirming the concept of the *umma*. As Khaled Abou El Fadl (1994:165) points out, it has been standard juridical, theological and socio-political Islamic practice to assert that 'all Muslims belong to a single community...regardless of their residence'. This jurisprudential tradition has been reinvigorated by contemporary politics. As Cesari (2003:257) herself acknowledges, young European Muslims are in some cases turning to the notion of the *umma* both to express a sense of Islamic identity that is seen as free from 'national or ethnic traditions' and as an identity structure that carries a clear statement of solidarity with Muslims abroad.

The increased articulation of Muslim solidarity can be attributed to two major factors. Firstly, a strengthening of reactive transnational identities as a response to the identity-stripping experience of globalisation and, secondly, the influence of new technology, such as the internet, which has enabled the emergence of 'virtual' communities that create a sense of unity that is not dependent on geographic proximity. The potential for competition or tension between a sense of transnational Muslim affiliation and support for the British state has been an increasing consideration for the British Muslim community. Indeed, given the contemporary political climate, there simply exists greater potential for these tensions to emerge. However, Muslims in Britain have been active participants in the social, cultural and political discourse of their state for decades. This engagement was merely thrown into sharper relief in the era of the 'war on terror', a period in which British Muslims overwhelmingly opposed the terrorist attacks of 11 September 2001, but were also strongly opposed to the responses of Washington and London, especially the invasions of Afghanistan and Iraq.

Unravelling the identity structure of British Muslims thus requires an appreciation of the interplay of various influences, loyalties, rights and responsibilities. Ramadan (1999:116) affirms that identity is a mixture of 'feelings, emotions, state of mind, cultures and customs'. It is an intensely personal discourse, and is influenced by a broad range of factors. Similarly, for the minority of British Muslims who elect to follow an Islamist course, the decision-making process is part of both a broader political context and a personal set of circumstances.

Al-Muhajiroun was a manifestation of Islamism in the United Kingdom. In order to clearly situate this organisation within the broader movement it is instructive to consider the history and primary tenets of international Islamism.

Notes

1 Information from the 2000 Index of Multiple Deprivation, cited in UKFCO (2004).
2 Other sources place this higher, around 11% of the community as a whole (see An-Na'im 2006:38).
3 Results from Family Resources Survey, Department for Work and Pensions 2000/01, cited in White (2002:10).
4 Results from Family Resources Survey, Department for Work and Pensions 2000/01 cited in White (2002:9).
5 Results from the 2000 British Crime Survey (Home Office Research Study 223), cited in White (2002:13).
6 For a more detailed analysis see Baxter (2006a).
7 In the mid-1980s a British secondary school head teacher became embroiled in a public showdown with the Muslim community in Bradford. In response to the changing ethnic demographic of his school, Honeyford published a series of inflammatory articles questioning the prevailing doctrine of multiculturalism in the classroom (Halstead 1988; Honeyford 1982:20–21; 1983; 1984; 1986:35;). The 'Honeyford affair', as the saga became known, was a precursor to the infamous Rushdie affair of the late 1980s and illuminated similar issues of community activism and identity assertion.
8 Khomeini's broadcast on Tehran Radio quoted in MacDonogh, The Rushdie Letters, 130.

part two

Contextualising Islamism

Islamism is as a multifaceted political movement that claims to have Islam as its nucleus. It encompasses a broad swath of viewpoints and organisations, including those that reject violence as a means of achieving societal change. The primary challenge in defining the term Islamism is a simple question: whose Islam? As with any religion, the interpretation of the individual believer, let alone those of a broad range of sectarian groups, national and ethnic communities and organisations means an all-encompassing definition of Islam is challenging enough. Following this, a clear definition of a political movement whose adherents claim to act in the 'name' of Islam becomes even more difficult.

As a movement, Islamism enjoyed a degree of internal coherence within the Muslim world in the mid- to late 20th century. Modern Islamism was strongly influenced by earlier traditions, including the Salafi movement which emerged as a trend in Sunni Islam in the late-18th century. In this period, Salafi reformers sought to transform their communities, believing 'that only by going back to the origin of the religion as it was revealed to the Prophet would a more just and righteous society appear' (Fattah 2003:131). At its origins, Salafism was a reactive trend that aimed to cleanse Islam of increasing Sufi tendencies that were seen as polytheistic. The movement referred to the experience of the Prophet and the *as-salaf as-salih* (the first three generations) as the ultimate blueprint for a Muslim society. In this way, initially, Salafism could be understood as a reformist and largely egalitarian movement. Salafism advocated the empowerment of the individual within religion and many Salafis focused on the right of the individual to personally interpret the texts of Islam. Importantly, the Salafi movement has never constituted a unified international organisation. Rather the tradition has sparked the development of individual organisations that exist throughout the Middle East, Southeast Asia and the West. Salafism then, refers to a worldview to which individuals or organisations choose to adhere.

The most famous offshoot of the Salafi tradition came to prominence only as a result of a certain set of political, economic and social circumstances. The Wahhabi doctrine is derived from the teachings of Muhammad 'Abd al-

Wahhab (1703–87), an Arabian preacher who drew his inspiration from the jurist Taqi al-Din Ahmad Ibn Taymiyya (1263–1328). Al-Wahhab formulated his ideas as a response to the experience of Ottoman rule, thus from its very origins Wahhabism includes elements of political rejection. Al-Wahhab sought to cleanse Islam of what he viewed as corruptions and impurities such as 'mysticism, intercession, intellectualism, sectarianism and rationalism in order to restore its pristine purity' (Hassan 2007:13). Essentially, the preacher sought to de-emphasise the cultural elements that had been incorporated and enabled the rapid geographic transmission of the faith. Al-Wahhab's alliance with the al-Saud tribe in Central Arabia led to a fusion of tribal military strength and literalist religion that lay latent for a century and a half and then spectacularly emerged under the leadership of Abd al-'Aziz bin Sa'ud. Under his charismatic leadership, the application of Wahhabism to the region of Central Arabia led to the unification of tribal forces and the formation of the modern state of Saudi Arabia (Bubalo & Fealy 2005:12). This literal and marginal interpretation of Islam became the governing creed of the Kingdom. However, it is important to note that the Salafi tradition had many manifestations (Fattah 2003:132). Contemporary Salafism was, like numerous other movements in the developing world, greatly impacted by the historical experience of colonial domination. According to Riaz Hassan,

> Salafism is an intellectual response that developed fully under the conditions of post-colonial Muslim societies whose governments failed to deliver the fruits of the 'national project' ie jobs, economic development, welfare for its citizens and equality of citizenship (Hassan 2007:14).

This is supported by Mohammed Ayoob, who suggests the colonial experience undercut the traditional hierarchies of authority in Muslim societies, leaving the field open to laythinkers, individuals not trained in traditional seminaries, to interpret the faith (Ayoob 2005). The Saudi Arabian experience is distinct as, unlike the broader Middle East, the Saudi Kingdom did not experience colonial domination. Thus, Salafism as it developed in the Saudi Arabian context did not have the anti-colonial undertones which characterise much Islamic thinking in the early 20th century. Furthermore, as Bubalo and Fealy warn, the Saudi Arabian derivative should be 'viewed as a distinct form of Salafism given that it is not just an approach to religion but also, in effect, a state ideology' (Bubalo & Fealy 2005:39).

The Saudi Kingdom's economic windfall in the 1970s facilitated the global dissemination of a version of the Salafi tradition that had largely merged with the Wahhabi doctrine. Saudi money flowed into mosques throughout the Muslim world and the West, bringing with it preachers indoctrinated in this worldview. This co-option of the Salafi tradition by the proponents of Wahhabism has not been without critique.[1] Moreover, this Saudi-backed trend was only one element in the diverse Islamist movement which emerged in the 20th century.

In the 'revival' period of the 1950s–70s, the modern Islamist movement was pioneered by three thinkers, the Muslim Brotherhood's Sayyid Qutb, the subcontinent's Abu al-A'la Mawdudi and the Iranian Ayatollah, Rudollah Khomeini. These thinkers advocated differing interpretations of Islam and hailed from both sides of the Sunni/Shia divide, yet they all interpreted Islam as a revolutionary doctrine capable of affecting powerful social and political change. As is the case with all movements, Islamism did not emerge in an intellectual or ideological vacuum. Thus, while it was an indigenous response to the experience of the Muslim world, Islamism was greatly affected by international political trends. As Henry Munson (2003:40) suggests, a central irony of modern Islamism is that while the movement largely rejected nation-state divisions in the Muslim Middle East it demonstrated clear nationalistic tendencies, calling for a nationalism based on the regional, and even universal 'nation' of Islam.

Modern Islamism emerged in response to the realities of the 20th century. The Muslim Brotherhood, founded by the Egyptian teacher Hassan al-Banna in 1928, is a clear example of this. The Muslim Brotherhood's agenda had distinct anti-colonial overtones and was focused on the Islamisation of society through grassroots activism and education. As the Egyptian state increased its repression leading proponents, such as Sayyid Qutb (1906–1966), radicalised their views. This symbiotic relationship between repression and radicalisation is a common theme in Islamist politics. Therefore, Islamism was, in part, a response to the socio-political context of its proponents. For example, Qutb's thinking was clearly and definitively a product of his historical epoch, the period of Arab nationalism. Qutb's greatest innovation was his understanding of the concept of *jahiliyya*, a term that refers to the period preceding the revelation of Islam. Usually translated as meaning a period of 'ignorance' or 'barbarism', this concept is prevalent in the work of many theorists throughout Islamic history. In a demonstration of the interplay between theorists in this period, Mawdudi utilised this concept in relation to the Western and communist worlds (Shepard 2003:523). However, Qutb applied this concept to the secular-nationalist political climate of Egypt and the broader Middle East. Yet, as an advocate of Islamic revivalism, Qutb also appealed to the ethos of nationalism. He interpreted the concept expansively, advocating the global nationhood of humanity. At its core, Qutb's thinking was based on the universal applicability of Islam (Khatab 2004:217). The question of universalism versus nationalism was a key theme for the revivalist thinkers and it was played out in different ways.

For example, Islamic universality was also present in Khomeini's thinking. However, Khomeini's experience was framed by the need for practical governance of a state. Therefore, over time, his universalist understandings were submerged in the success of the nationalist revolution in Iran. Munson (2003:43) agrees that Khomeini was 'in fact passionately attached to the nation of Iran, despite his opposition to nationalism as ideology'. This is indicative of the often contradictory trends that permeate Islamist doctrine. As Roy (1999:202) points out, despite the universalist pretensions of the rhetoric of the Islamic Revolution, in Iran 'the status and role of religion is nevertheless defined by political institutions, not religious ones', or more emphatically, as politics was linked to the nation-state, 'politics rules over religion'. This theme was also present in Mawdudi's thought. Mawdudi's writings at the time of the establishment of Pakistan embraced nationalism as the means to 'mould Pakistan into the perfect Islamic state' (Idris 2003:548). Moreover, Mawdudi strongly asserted that Muslims could not accept minority status, a position that also reflected the time and place in which he was operating (Bonney 2004:208). This demonstrates the inherently politicised nature of Mawdudi's theological perspective, a perspective in which religion was utilised to advocate the creation of a new state on the subcontinent.

The Islamist movement's focus on universalism quickly led to a need to consider the relationship between Muslims and the non-Muslim world. Again, these three thinkers were influenced by their individual historical contexts. Mawdudi's thought focused on the binary relationship between Islam and the West, a relationship that he understood as one of diametric opposition. In Qutb's worldview the focus is different. Despite the latter utilisation of his work by organisations which were overtly anti-Western, it can be suggested that Qutb's thought was more clearly a response to the role of Arab/Muslim leaders vis-á-vis their own societies. The radicalisation of Qutb's views during his years of incarceration supports this contention.

In Khomeini's case, the theme of anti-Western sentiment as a consequence of domestic considerations is also evident. It can be argued that the central role anti-Americanism came to play in Khomeini's rhetoric was strongly influenced by two factors. Firstly, US support for the deposed Shah and secondly, a reaction to the unpredicted radicalising influence of the hostage crisis in Tehran. Once the limited scope of Khomeini's revolution became apparent, anti-Western rhetoric was a useful propaganda tool to secure his position inside Iran. In Mawdudi's thinking, however, the anti-Western focus appears to be embedded. Once again the responsive nature of this worldview is clear as Mawdudi's immediate experience of colonialism shaped his perspective.

These three thinkers operated independently, yet can be seen as part of a broad impulse in the mid-20th century Muslim world which encouraged individuals and organisations to call for dramatic and lasting social and political change. These thinkers drew on an entwined tradition of political and theological thought and adapted the doctrines of their faith to form the basis of revolutionary socio-political movements. As Mawdudi asserted, in this mindset, 'Islam is not merely a religious creed...It is a comprehensive system which seeks to annihilate all evil and tyrannical systems in the world and enforce its own programme of reform' (Bonney 2004:204).

The interplay between the theological and the political are hallmarks of the Islamist movement. As stated, modern Islamism developed in response to specific socio-political challenges in the Middle East during the 20th century, and therefore, historical exploration offers some assistance in building a workable understanding of this movement. Numerous Islamist organisations have been explored by academics and the media in recent years. The focus of this study, al-Muhajiroun, emerged from the global organisation of Hizb al-Tahrir. Considering this, it is instructive to explore the historical experiences of this organisation, before turning to an investigation of the concept of jihad.

Hizb al-Tahrir

The establishment of the State of Israel in 1948 provided the catalyst for a period of Arab political, social and religious upheaval that continues to this day. Amid the range of responses that the new state invoked or solidified, Islamism proved the most resilient and confronting. As the Arab world grappled with the emergence of the Jewish state, the displacement of the Palestinians and the failure of the Arab military response, the prevailing political response was Arab nationalism. A leading proponent of this trend was the Ba'th party, which was formalised in Syria in 1946. However, the Ba'th party and other secular-nationalist organisations minimised an element of the Arab tradition, the transformative power of Islam. The embryonic history of al-Muhajiroun can be seen as a contemporary manifestation of the process that began with the activists who sought to restore Islam to the forefront of Arab political responses to modernity. Al-Muhajiroun's parent organisation, Hizb al-Tahrir, was formed in East Jerusalem in the early 1950s by Taqi al-Din Nabhani (1909–77). Nabhani trained as a teacher of Islamic law and was employed within the local court system in the late 1930s. Like many other university-educated young men of his generation, he was drawn to the Ba'th platform and its potential for Arab renewal (Devlin 1976:41). Nabhani became active in Ba'thist circles in the closing years of the 1940s, a period dominated by conflict and the establishment of Israel.

The Ba'th movement was similar to contemporaneous Western revolutionary doctrines. Its appeal was its positive promotion of Arab identity, underscored by the importance of history, language and unity (Omar 1996). According to William L Cleveland (2000:316), the party was committed to ending 'social injustice, class exploitation, and tyranny and to establish(ing) freedom, democracy and socialism'. Additionally, the Ba'th Party called for a revolutionary vanguard to overhaul the Arab political structure. For Nabhani a strong belief in Arab unity did not prevent increasing questions regarding the secondary value which the Ba'thists attached to religion.

In this period, Arab political unification was the foremost concern of many regional thinkers. For some, the establishment of Israel and the subsequent Arab military defeats were seen as a result of the earlier loss of the Islamic political unit, the Caliphate. Numerous scholars have noted the immense impact that the dissolution of the Caliphate had upon Islamic and Arab thinkers of this period. As Suha Taji-Farouki asserts, Nabhani was no exception to this trend (Farouki 1996:x). By 1952, Nabhani's critique of the Ba'thist tendency to relegate religion to a minor role within Arab politics had developed into outright rejection of the party and its doctrine of largely secular renewal. In many ways, Nabhani's political activism reveals the intersecting trends prevalent in the Arab world at this time. While often presented as a disaffected Ba'thist, some scholars suggest Nabhani was part of the Muslim Brotherhood and thus categorise his nascent organisation as an offshoot of the regional movement (Naumkin 2005:128; Bubalo & Fealy 2005:38).

Leaving the Ba'th Party, Nabhani focused on religion as the foundation of Arab identity and presented it as the core of the Arab nation. The central tenet of Nabhani's thought, and the defining feature of the movements he pioneered, was the determination to re-establish the Caliphate. This focus reveals a fundamentally religious worldview. Nabhani positioned himself in this paradigm, asserting that the Caliphate was the only legitimate political system for the Arab world and the key to the restoration of Islam as a global power. This doctrine, a rejection of the imported system of nation-states and thus by extension its imposer, the West, often encouraged adherents to adopt a confrontational position. However, Nabhani sought to purify the Arab community by re-focusing it, through Islam, on the achievements of its own cultural and political heritage. In this the influence of the Muslim Brotherhood, with its tradition of grassroots activism, may well be evident.

In the early 1950s, Nabhani consolidated his followers into a political party and attempted to register it with the Jordanian authorities that controlled East Jerusalem. However, in 1952 and again in 1953 his applications for registration were rejected (Farouki 1996:7). Considering the pan-Islamic aspirations of the party and its endorsement of a political system that would fundamentally negate the legitimacy of the Hashemite monarchy, this is not surprising.[2] More broadly, the Jordanian government maintained a difficult relationship with most fledgling Palestinian political movements, many of which challenged the legitimacy of Amman's rule. Nabhani, determined to emphasise the religious nature of his organisation, based the party in Jerusalem. Despite a series of arrests in 1953, Hizb al-Tahrir was eventually registered as a political party in mid-June 1954 (Staloff 1994:92). Once the party's legal status was assured it occasionally attempted to engage with the existing political structure through the local electoral process. However, Hizb al-Tahrir remained true to its origins as a secret society and preferred to disseminate its message through study circles and grassroots activities.

Hizb al-Tahrir's influence grew beyond Palestinian towns and communities and the organisation soon developed support bases in Amman and Beirut.[3] However, Hizb al-Tahrir proved unable to effectively challenge the dominant regional movement of pan-Arabism, spearheaded by the charismatic Egyptian President Gamal Abd al-Nasser. Ideologically, Nabhani's organisation diverged from other regional political responses in its expansive worldview. While spawned in the mire of 1940s Palestinian politics, Hizb al-Tahrir focus was the restoration of the Caliphate. This agenda is indicative of the interplay between various movements and doctrines in this period. For example, Hizb al-Tahrir's ideology is reminiscent of the Ba'thist focus on the need for Arab unity. However, as a point of divergence, Nabhani choose to expand 'the borders of an ephemeral hyperstate from the Arab...to the Islamic world' (Naumkin 2005:129). In this way, Hizb al-Tahrir followed a vision that responded to, yet simultaneously transcended, regional politics.

In response to the omnipresent question of Israel, Hizb al-Tahrir developed a clear, if unusual, perspective. While engaging directly with the plight of the Palestinian people, Hizb al-Tahrir rejected a state-based solution. Palestinians were thus encouraged to wait for the restoration of the Caliphate, dismiss all attempts at resolution and cling to the 'right of return'. The Palestinian plight is usually understood as a nationalist conflict. Therefore, this anti-nationalist reading of the Palestinian situation distinguished Hizb al-Tahrir in its cultural and political milieu. In a political context marked by conflict, Hizb al-Tahrir publicly rejected political violence. However, the determination to endorse the Caliphate as the sole legitimate political construct for Muslims constituted a clear challenge to the ruling Arab elites whose power was directly derived from and enshrined in the state system. This led to Hizb al-Tahrir's eventual prohibition throughout the region. Despite sporadic influence in Jordan and Southern Iraq in the 1960s and 1970s, the organisation suffered in terms of external impact and internal cohesion, a trend that culminated in a loss of effective direction after the death of Nabhani in 1977.

However, the driving ideological basis of the party, the re-establishment of the Caliphate, proved a difficult concept to suppress. The failure of pan-Arabism, the corruption that characterised a range of regional leaderships and a general sense of decline pervaded the Arab world. Activists from across the spectrum of Arab politics began to question whether the faith they had shown in state-based nationalism as a successor to the disintegration of Islamic political power had been misguided. As Israeli military dominance and Western influence was repeatedly reinforced, the younger generations sought an authentic response. In a trend that began in the aftermath of the 1967 Arab–Israeli war, and intensified as a result of the Iranian Revolution of 1979, many turned to Islam and called for its restoration at the heart of regional politics. Hizb al-Tahrir leaders, often from a Sunni background, largely welcomed the establishment of the Islamic Republic in Iran. Indeed, some claim that Hizb al-Tahrir, although largely disenfranchised at this time, was so enamoured with the events in Tehran that a delegation was sent inviting the Ayatollah Khomeini to become the new Caliph.[4] This view is supported by researchers who suggest the Iranian notion of *vilayat-e faqih* (rule of the jurist) is, despite the historical antagonism of Hizb al-Tahrir towards the Shia Islam, not dissimilar to the focused call for Islamic unification under a Caliph that characterises the Hizb al-Tahrir vision (Naumkin 2005:134). While this was clearly an unrealistic initiative it did reveal the inspirational power of the Iranian Revolution and the strong desire within the organisation to transform the prevailing system of governance in the region, even at the expense of traditional sectarian divides. Similar to the many Islamic organisations spawned in this period, Hizb al-Tahrir increasingly interpreted Islamic tradition in a literal fashion. The party viewed the Prophet Muhammad's life as the blueprint for Islamic society and the linking of this concept to the idea of the Caliphate as the only legitimate political Muslim structure came to characterise the now largely underground organisation.

Surviving its prohibition in the Middle East, Hizb al-Tahrir experienced re-birth in a range of geographical contexts. This suggests its ideological and theological premises were popular and transferable to ethnically and culturally distinct parts of the Muslim world. Nabhani's vision of Muslim, as opposed to Arab unity, gave the party currency in regions untouched by the experience of Nasserism. In particular, the break-up of the Soviet Union in the 1990s provided a new opportunity.[5] Muslim Central Asia proved fertile ground for a political program based on Islam. Vitaly Naumkin identifies a central obstacle in the study of Hizb al-Tahrir with his assertion that the underground nature of the party's leadership hierarchy in Central Asia complicates clear analysis of the organisation's history in the region (Naumkin 2005:127). This said, it is widely accepted that the party appeared first in Uzbekistan and then emerged in the neighbouring states of Kyrgyzstan and Tajikistan. The on-going relevance of the movement's notion of Muslim unity was also evident in its appearance in ever-more diverse regions. For example, Hizb al-Tahrir also gained a presence in Indonesia. However, Bubalo and Fealy caution that the emergence of Islamist perspectives in the Asian world is due to a range of factors, including an indigenous minority tradition of radicalism. Focusing on external influences, they suggest three major trends have assisted the spread of Islamism in Indonesia: human movement between Indonesia and the Arab Middle East (including Indonesia participation in the conflict in Afghanistan in the 1980s), Middle Eastern (particularly Saudi Arabian) propagation in the region and, finally, publishing and the internet (Bubalo & Fealy 2005:49).

In addition to the Central Asian and Asian contexts, Hizb al-Tahrir sought influence within the Muslim Diaspora. Branches of the organisation emerged throughout Western Europe, particularly in Germany and, as will be explored, the United Kingdom. Today, Hizb al-Tahrir continues to operate under a shroud of secrecy. Therefore, the internet has become an invaluable tool. The party maintains a website that allows for the dissemination of its doctrine, while also affording anonymity to its leadership. In line with its theoretical beginnings, Hizb al-Tahrir continues to identify as a political party with Islam as its ideology. As an organisation formulated within the Islamic world, and aimed predominately at internal reform, its global expansion posed new challenges. In relation to the organisation's doctrine, the position of Western Muslims was highly problematic. The contradictions in Muslim citizens of established Western nation-states endorsing a return to a pan-Islamic political structure are evident. However, Hizb al-Tahrir still emerged as a minority movement among Western Muslims, effectively completing the transition from a Middle Eastern organisation to a globalised movement. The organisation remains characterised by the belief that a re-establishment of the Caliphate in Muslim-majority regions is vital and its Western branches claim to work towards that eventuality. However, the final conclusion of the Hizb al-Tahrir struggle purports a greater goal. Hizb al-Tahrir identifies itself as initially adhering to the dual aim of conveying the Islamic message to the world and purifying the existing Muslim community. Ideally, both these aims can be best achieved under the agency of an Islamic state, premised on the Shariah and conducted in line with the historic experience of the Caliphate. However, the universalist intentions of the organisation are unmistakeable.

The Party...aims at the correct revival of the Ummah through enlightened thought. It also strives to bring her back to her previous might and glory such that she wrests the reins of initiative away from other states and nations, and returns to her rightful place as the first state in the world, as she was in the past, when she governs the world according to the laws of Islam. It also aims to bring back the Islamic guidance for mankind and to lead the Ummah into a struggle with *Kufr*, its systems and its thoughts so that Islam encapsulates the world.[6]

Hizb al-Tahrir identifies two primary foci in its struggle: Western colonialist states and the Arab leaderships that it identifies as failing to govern in accordance with Islam. In this it draws on the thinking of Islamist thinkers such as Qutb and Mawdudi. However, Hizb al-Tahrir eschews violence as a tool to affect social and political change. In order to legitimise this call for non-violent agitation, Hizb al-Tahrir cites the example of the Prophet's restraint in the Meccan period of early Islamic history. Despite this, the organisation's doctrines of Muslim unity and the rejection of nationalist divisions in the Muslim world constitute a marked challenge to the legitimacy of state-based regimes, especially in the Middle East. Logically, the fulfilment of the Hizb al-Tahrir vision of a restored Caliphate in a region in which the existence of nation-state system is irrefutable is unlikely without recourse to violence. This tension is revealed as Hizb al-Tahrir still regularly clashes with government authority in the Muslim world. The party acknowledges this struggle, claiming 'the oppressive rulers in Iraq, Syria, Libya and others have killed dozens of (our) members. The prisons of Jordan, Syria, Iraq, Egypt, Libya and Tunisia are full of (our) members.'[7] It is this ill-defined relationship between political violence and the universialist aims which has significantly complicated the organisation's existence in both the Middle East and the West.

Globalising Islamism: the impact of Afghanistan

The development of Islamism, as represented by Hizb al-Tahrir, is clearly a result of experiences within the Muslim world. Yet, like all Islamist organisations, Hizb al-Tahrir was indirectly affected by the events in Afghanistan in the 1980s. As the revival period came to a close, the Islamist movement swayed from its initial focus on internal reform. The Afghan experience, with its instrumentalisation of Islam as the basis of modern militant resistance irrevocably altered this movement. Islamism became increasingly diffuse and unfocused, anti-Western sentiment becoming its predominant characteristic. However, the roots of this disintegration may be embedded in the 20th-century experience itself. Historically, Islamism encompassed tensions between the conflicting legacies of Khomeini, the theologian, and Qutb, the political dissident. These two trends, the theological and the political, are evident throughout the Islamic tradition. It may be the case that these two agendas were thrown into sharp relief as the movement became prevalent outside the context of intra-Muslim politics.

Modern Islamism entered the international political sphere through the Muhajideen resistance to the Soviet occupation of Afghanistan in 1979. As volunteers flooded into the region to participate, a globalising of Islamist doctrines occurred. This mind-set, sharpened by the experience of combat against an occupying super-power, then spread through the Muslim world and beyond. During the 1990s, militant Islamism was carried throughout the international system by the veterans of this lengthy conflict (Saeed 2002:84). Moreover, in this period, transnational militant Islamist organisations that perpetrated or advocated a mindset of violence against their perceived enemies also emerged.

In this way, the Soviet invasion of a troubled Central Asian state set the scene for the globalisation of militant Islamism. However, while external actors such as the Soviet Union played a role, the experience of Afghanistan merely brought together the various Islamist trends of the mid-20th century. As Roy (2005:364) points out, 'the main motivation for [Islamist] radicalisation is not theological [instead] political radicalisation is the main driving force'. Thus, modern Islamism is *a political* movement that gained prominence in the Muslim world as the ideologies of the 20th century (nationalism, socialism, secularism) faltered. Islamist doctrines were initially advocated by activists seeking to transform their own societies. Following the conflict in Afghanistan, it could be argued that Islamism moved away from its origins as a program of socio-political transformation and devolved into an expression of political rejectionism and violence that was constructed and legitimised through the use of Islamic imagery, concepts and terminology.

Into this process stepped Hizb al-Tahrir, and its offshoot al-Muhajiroun, both of which endorsed a form of 'Muslim identity stripped of any particular cultural or national context' (Bubalo & Fealy 2005:38). This notion of literally 'globalised' Islamic identity is highly adaptable as it does not rely on the confines of geographic location, or indeed local historical and cultural norms. This proved appealing to a minority of British Muslims. In the case of Western Muslims, the potential for pre-disposition to Islamism may pivot on a range of factors. The perception of the Muslim place in British society as marginalised and the (usually second and third generation) lack of identification with their land of ancestry may play a part in explaining the appeal of a universalised structure of identity. The increased suffering of Muslims in the international system and, by virtue of enhanced technology, a greater exposure to that suffering, may also be relevant. In a linked point, the determination to conflagrate international realities with local socio-political experiences is significant. Finally, a reactive determination to position a highly politicised interpretation of Islam as the basis of identity may be the outcome. As Islamism gained influence outside the context of the Muslim world, adaptation was required. Activists were now operating outside the Muslim world's socio-political environment, an environment in which they had been able to focus their activities upon the role of 'unjust' or 'un-Islamic' leaderships. Therefore, the movement was forced to find new points of definition and unity. The contested notion of jihad emerged as a major rallying point for the post-Afghanistan, globalised, Islamist movement.

A brief history of jihad

The concept of jihad has numerous meanings, and any definition is largely dependent on historical time, place and agenda. Put simply, jihad means different things to different people. As Saeed (2002:74) points out, throughout history interpretations of the doctrine have ranged from 'totally non-violent to violent actions'. This is part of the dualistic strength and weakness of the doctrine of jihad within Islam. Varied interpretations, all with textual legitimacy, can be drawn from the annals of Islamic history. Thus, the doctrine is largely open to interpretation and (mis)representation and this is part of its appeal to Islamist organisations.

In the Islamic tradition there exists a notion of a greater and lesser jihad. Contemporary researchers, among them Larbi Sadiki (1995), assert that the 'lesser' jihad of physical, often military, action is not as important as the 'greater' jihad of 'spiritual, political, social, economic and intellectual forms of struggle'. It is acknowledged that non-militant interpretations of jihad are plentiful in the contemporary Muslim world. However, at other times in Islamic history Muslims, often as a result of their historical and political situations, have understood the concept in more militaristic terms. For example, the need to entrench the existence of the early Islamic community led many thinkers and jurists to focus on the 'lesser' jihad of physical or military action.

The delineation of jihad into offensive and defensive categories was another feature of the classical period. Offensive jihad came to be understood as actions taken to 'propagate the religion, to make it triumph and to intimidate the enemy', while defensive jihad was seen as fighting 'out of necessity...in defence of the religion, of things that are inviolable, and of lives' (Peters 1996:51–2). In the contemporary period, modernist thinkers who advocate the demilitarisation of this concept have often affirmed defensive action as the only legitimate application of physical jihad. Saeed (2002:81) supports this, stating that the idea of the 'purely defensive jihad...gained ground in the twentieth century'.

The physical or militant concept of jihad has become central to the ideological platform of militant Islamism. Overall, the concept of jihad plays a pivotal role within contemporary Islamic politics. It has emerged as the primary battle ground for the intellectual and ideological struggle between reformists and Islamists. This debate has become more intense as international politics has provided various conflict scenarios which may well fulfil even the modernist interpretation of a legitimate 'defensive' call to jihad. It is argued here that the traditional distinctions of offensive and defensive jihad have become blurred within the contemporary Islamist mindset, a development that has been assisted by the experiences of the 1980s and 1990s, and the political climate fostered by the 'war on terror'. However, the discourse surrounding jihad significantly pre-dates these events.

The three 'revival' theorists of Islamism, Qutb, Mawdudi and Khomeini, played a central role in the expansive interpretation of jihad that gained strength during the 20th century. These thinkers advocated the power of Islam as a revolutionary doctrine, and often identified jihad as the preferred methodology of societal transformation. In Qutb's paradigm, the role of jihad is to remove, or overthrow, the systems that prevent Islam from assuming its rightful place as a global system of governance. In this way, jihad is seen as an active undertaking. Overall, the revivalists leant 'strongly towards the expansionist doctrines' inherent in the concept of jihad (Copinger-Symes 2001:53). Saeed recognises the historical continuity of this perspective, asserting the dynamic and all-encompassing nature of jihad presented by the revivalist thinkers drew strongly on the legacy of the classical period, in which offensive jihad was literally a 'doctrine of war' (Saeed 2002:77). Indeed, well before the current industry of Islamic studies, Manoucher Parvin and Maurice Sommet (1980:4) noted that militant jihad 'remains a fact of history'. It is this militant interpretation of the notion of jihad which will be explored here.

Early constructions

The term jihad appears frequently in the Qur'an. Bernard Lewis suggests the Meccan phase of the revelation focused on jihad as a form of 'moral striving,' an understanding that forms the basis of the modernist interpretation, while in the Medina phase the notion of jihad held 'more explicitly practical connotations' (Lewis 2003:30). Warfare was vital to the early community's survival and expansion, therefore its inclusion and sanctification within Islamic tradition is not surprising. As mentioned, throughout early Islamic history, theorists developed the notion of two kinds of physical jihad, the defensive and the offensive categorisations. The defensive jihad is legitimised in the Qur'anic injunction, 'fight in the cause of God those who fight you, but do not transgress limits; for

God loveth not transgressors' (Qur'an 2:190). This sura affirms the right of the Muslim community to retaliate in the face of an attack; yet, it clearly stipulates the principle of proportionate response.

A focus on historical context and an increased inclination toward allegorical textual exegesis led many modernist thinkers to reject the legitimacy of armed jihad in the modern context. Such interpretations are dismissed by Islamist scholars and organisations that seek to emphasise the militant connotations of the concept. The Islamist viewpoint is also based on the Qur'an and utilises different suras that detail jihad as a clearly militant requirement.

> But when the forbidden months are past, then fight and slay the Pagans wherever ye find them, and seize them, beleaguer them, and lie in wait for them in every stratagem (of war); but if they repent, and establish regular prayers and practise regular charity, then open the way for them: for God is Oft-forgiving, Most Merciful (Qur'an 9:5).

As can be seen even from the two short passages detailed here, from a purely textual perspective, the interpretation and understanding of the Muslim duty of jihad is largely dependent on the Qur'anic passages that are emphasised and the intentions of those providing the interpretation.

After the death of the Prophet, interpretations of the Qur'anic concept of jihad were developed in response to, and in accordance with, the changing fortunes of the Islamic empire. In the early battles that served to establish the community, the notion of jihad was utilised as a paradigm within which to frame, justify and moderate conflict. Following this, the notion of jihad was developed to facilitate the established leadership's objective of expanding *dar al-Islam* (Batley 2003:12). James Turner Johnson affirms that the classical idea of jihad, and indeed the Islamic view of the world beyond Islam, was formulated 'in a climate where Islam was superior—militarily and intellectually—from a position of certainty and power' (Johnson 1997:68). Similarly, Rudolph Peters comments on the importance of the historical context, pointing out that 'the crux of the doctrine is the existence of one single Islamic state [which rules] the entire *umma*' (Peters 1996:3). This encapsulates the problematic nature of jihad in the modern world. The doctrine, as formulated in the first ten centuries of Islamic history, was premised and dependent upon the concept of a unified Islamic state. Given their historical experience, this was the only conceivable political reality for the thinkers of classical Islam. The historical doctrine was understood as the community, *as a unified entity*, undertaking defensive action to protect itself or—with the authorisation of a legitimate Islamic leadership (a caliph)—enacting offensive warfare to further its hegemonic aspirations. The concept of offensive jihad, as it was historically formulated, has limited relevance or legitimacy in the contemporary era, where the Islamic empire does not exist and therefore has no hegemonic power to project. Even the defensive application (war in response to an attack), which is traditionally understood as binding upon individual Muslims (Hashmi 2003:205), and thus potentially capable of circumventing the absence of legitimate leadership, is inherently complicated by the reality of nation-state affiliations and internal divisions, both religious and ideological, within the Muslim world.

This returns us to the central question: to what level do Muslims consciously identify as an *umma*? In this context, another question is suggested; does this intangible identification (which contradicts the political reality of the global order) constitute a basis from which a call to jihad, as it was historically formulated, can be made? Considering the above, the contemporary revival of the concept of jihad could be viewed as an attempt to apply a doctrine from a world that no longer exists. The reality of Muslim nation-states appears to render the historical doctrine of militant offensive jihad deeply problematic. However, regardless of the preferred methodology, the jihad doctrine functioned as a call for unity in the interests of the *umma*. This concept was not historically specific. Therefore, the jihad doctrine was reformulated as an expression of anti-secularism, and then anti-Western sentiment, in the mid-20th century. The majority of proponents substitute the formal Islamic entity with the *umma*, arguing that in a time marked by the absence of an Islamic state, the transnational community of believers function in its place. It is from this basis that a call for defensive jihad is made.

Jihad in the 20th century

As is the case across all religions, the experience of Islam is about more than faith and texts. The often brutal history of the Middle East in the 20th century played a significant role in how the notion of jihad developed and why it gained such a central role in contemporary Islamism. The influence of the 20th century is important, yet the contemporary radicalisation of the concept of jihad may find its roots in the thoughts of the jurist and legal philosopher Ibn Taymiyya (1263–1328), who developed the idea of warfare against the apostate Muslim ruler. Taymiyya elevated the role of jihad within the faith, presenting it as the 'the best voluntary (religious) act a man can perform.'[8] Taymiyya's innovation was the application of jihad, traditionally seen as military action to defend or expand the Islamic lands, *within* the domestic realm of the Muslim world. Shifting focus from the external world, Taymiyya claimed that jihad could and should be utilised to unseat Muslim rulers who failed to apply 'correct' Sharia.

This mindset was given new impetus in the early 20th century. The close of the First World War and the imperial domination of the Middle East revealed to many Arabs the inability of Muslim societies to resist the West, first militarily, then politically and, most devastatingly, culturally (Adams 1986:i). In order to arrest the decline of the Islamic world individuals and movements sought reform. Some reformers, such as Mustafa Kemal, viewed Islam as the barrier to the region's entry into the modern world. Kemal, with his focus on Turkish nationalism and Westernisation, declared that the Caliphate 'could only have been a laughing stock in the eyes of the civilised world'.[9] As the early-20th century's most powerful and successful regional proponent of secularisation, Kemal viewed Islam and modernity as irreconcilable. As Bobby S Sayyid (2003:59) points out, Kemal's abolishment of the Caliphate, the last vestige of Islamic unity spawned a range of responses. In a mid-20th century Arab world where secular-nationalism and socialism were struggling to deliver social justice or economic prosperity the theological traditions of men such as Taymiyya gained some relevance as a potential panacea to the troubled politics of the region. Moreover, the omnipresent West with its superior military capability and ability to enforce colonial rule was a constant reminder of Islam's dramatic reversal of fortune in the temporal world. Drawing on the historical legacy and energised by the dire political reality of the period, the reformulation of the concept of jihad occurred, in part as a political response to increasing secularisation and Westernisation.

In the mid-20th century, activists often called for militant jihad against the forces of secularisation in the Middle East. As mentioned, Qutb was a major force in this movement. Gillies Kepel points out that the fundamental directives of Qutb's thought, the identification of Islam as a political movement and the need for a re-establishment of the Islamic Caliphate, have informed Islamist organisations since the 1960s (Kepel 2003:23). In relation to the concept of jihad, Qutb's seminal work, *Milestones,* provides a clear program of application (Qutb 1978:ch 4). Qutb focused on the centrality of jihad to the system of Islam. Some observers, such as Dilip Hiro, have posited that Qutb was against violence (Hiro 1989:68). However, Qutb's writings on the role of Islam outside the Islamic heartlands appear to contradict such assertions.

For Qutb, jihad is about the expansion of the Islamic faith, which he views as the fundamental directive of the Qur'an. However, jihad cannot be directly applied against people or communities as the Qur'an states there is no compulsion in religion.[10]

> Thus jihad needs to be directed against the ruling structures that withhold from individuals the freedom to choose Islam. No political system or material power should put hindrances in the way of preaching Islam. It should leave every individual free to accept or reject it, and if someone wants to accept it, it should

not prevent him or fight against him. If someone does this, then it is the duty of Islam to fight him until either he is killed or until he declares his submission (Qutb 1978:101–2).

In this way, Qutb formulates Islam as a revolutionary doctrine that seeks to overthrow the existing political system; as such this doctrine can be contextualised in the Egyptian political scene of the 1960s. In response to modernist interpretations of Islam that minimised the need for an offensive application of physical jihad, Qutb was direct:

> Islam is not a 'defensive movement' in the narrow sense that today is technically called a 'defensive war.' This narrow meaning is ascribed to it by those who are under the pressure of circumstances and are defeated by the wily attacks of the orientalists, who distort the concept of Islamic Jihaad. It was a movement to wipe out tyranny and to introduce true freedom to mankind (Qutb 1978:110–11).

As explored, Qutb clearly stressed Islamic universalism. 'Indeed, Islam has the right to take the initiative. Islam is not a heritage of any particular race or country; this is God's religion and it is for the whole world' (Qutb 1978:136). The rejection of Islam, or the legitimate realm of Islam, as territorially defined was an important feature of Qutb's thought.[11] This point, that for Qutb the *watan* (homeland) was borderless, has also been made by modern scholars such as Australia's Sayed Khatab (2004:219). In a linked point, Parvin and Sommet posit that this is the true historical understanding of the Islamic worldview, territorial understandings emerging only in response to Western contact (Parvin & Sommet 1980:15).

As Qutb's understanding of Islam was universalist, his application of jihad, by extension, carried the same interpretation. In this way Islam, as a revolutionary doctrine, became directed not just at the local regimes and leaderships but at all secular leadership worldwide. Esposito suggests that to Qutb and his predecessor Hasan al-Banna, 'the task of modern Muslims is nothing less than a great jihad against the enemies of Islam' (Esposito 1991:136). Esposito's perspective is perhaps based on Qutb's statements regarding the need for Islam to enter the global arena,

> ...with preaching as well as the movement, and to strike hard at all those political powers which force people to bow before them and which rule over them, unmindful of the commandments of God, and which prevent people from listening to the preaching and accepting the belief if they wish to do so (Qutb 1978:108–9).

To El Fadl, Qutb's thought reflects the 'simultaneous influences and contradictions of puritanical Islam, which were Salafism, Wahhabism and Western thought' (El Fadl 2005:82). This contemporary Islamic scholar rejects the sum total of Qutb's contribution as 'an attempt to add an Islamic veneer to a thoroughly fascist ideological construct.' A major player in the modern politicisation of Islam, Qutb's radical position owed much to his temporal circumstances. As mentioned, Qutb did spend time in the United States in the early 1950s and was shocked by what he perceived as a society consumed by 'materialism, racism and apparent sexual permissiveness' (Bonney 2004:215). However, it was during his decade-long incarceration in Nasser's jails that his writings reflect a hardening of perspectives and a clearer call for action. Indeed, given his suffering and eventual execution at the hands of the state it is not surprising that Qutb's worldview as it developed during his prison terms (1954–64 and then 1965–66) was characterised by a fierce rejection of the existing national leadership. Indeed, Qutb's position took him beyond the organisation with which his name has become synonymous. As El Fadl points out, Qutb's obsession with the practice of *takfir* (the act of accusing other Muslims of apostasy) was unpopular even within his own organisation, and the Muslim Brotherhood's official leadership at the time articulated concerns that Qutb's writings contradicted the Islamic tradition of tolerance (El Fadl 2005:84).

Despite the apparent concerns of the Muslim Brotherhood's leadership, Qutb's writings were further popularised in the aftermath of his execution in 1966. While not participating in militant action himself, Qutb can be seen as the theoretical forefather of the contemporary Islamist notion of jihad as recourse against the West. Qutb was not a trained Islamic scholar; rather, similar to those who followed his example, he captured a historical moment in which an inherently politicised reformulation of Islam was accepted by disenchanted sections of the Muslim world. Arguably, Qutb's worldview and popularity was only enhanced by the response of the Egyptian state. The power of Qutb's legacy was to become evident in the early 1980s, with the publication *Al-Faridah al-Ghaibah* (*The neglected duty*). This leaflet was published by the Egyptian Islamic Jihad organisation that was linked to the assassination of President Anwar Sadat in the aftermath of the 1979 Egyptian–Israeli peace accords.[12] The document, as an authentic treatise from inside the movement, offers insight into the late-20th century Islamist deliberations upon jihad and its application. While this understanding of jihad was legitimised through interpretation of certain passages in the Qur'an, its application as a mode of political resistance needs to be viewed in the context of the broader Islamist movement, which is a product of modernity. Johannes JG Jansen views the Islamic Jihad text as similar to Qutb's *Milestones*, both texts were an affirmation of militant jihad and a rejection of the Islamic scholars of the time who were seeking to emphasise non-militant interpretations of jihad (Jansen 1986:188). Esposito supports this view, stating that *The neglected duty* presents 'jihad as the sixth pillar of Islam'

(Esposito 1999:134). Within the document attempts at allegorical interpretation are rejected, as jihad is understood as 'fighting, which means confrontation and blood' (Jansen 1986:192). This interpretation, far removed from the modernist idea of an internal struggle, demonstrates how central the understandings of jihad became in Muslim politics, with modernists and Islamists struggling over the doctrine's interpretation and relevance. Furthermore, in the context of the early 1980s, the creeping secularisation of Muslim societies that galvanised Qutb was still of fundamental concern to the Islamist movement. Consequently, the focus of the movement was still largely *internal*, and the call to jihad was made in the hope of affecting change within the Muslim world itself. Similar to the Qutb model, within the mindset of Egyptian Islamic Jihad, any attempt to avoid or minimise the concept of militant jihad is a manifestation of the failure of Islamic identity and history in the post-Caliphate period. To adherents of this worldview, militant jihad is central to the system of Islam. Therefore, the failure to apply it is identified as a 'cause of the lowness, humiliation, division and fragmentation in which Muslims live' (Jansen 1986:205).

The 1980s Islamist reformulation of jihad can be seen as a tool in the struggle to reject secularisation and to prevent the dissolution of what is seen as the correct 'Islamic' historical, religious and social identity. In this way, jihad became the banner for resistance. The emphasis on jihad, the Islamic concept that can be least reconciled with the ethos of Westernisation and secularisation, demonstrated the Islamist determination to reconfigure Islam and Islamic identity in oppositional terms. These trends and impulses melded and evolved throughout the 1950–80 period, perhaps lacking a suitable proving ground. The conflict in Afghanistan in the 1980s enabled the intersection of these various influences in a paradigm of armed conflict against a Western state.

As Wiktorowicz (2001:22) points out, the Afghan conflict triggered new explorations of the religious justification for armed conflict by states (such as Saudi Arabia), organisations and individuals. The Soviet decision to invade Afghanistan in December 1979 would have lasting effects on international politics. Many of the individuals who travelled to fight the 'infidel' force of the Soviet Union subscribed to, or were indoctrinated in, a Salafi worldview that was funded and supported by the Wahhabi elite. From this particular set of political circumstances another variation on the Salafi-Wahhabi tradition emerged. Jihadist-Salafism finds its ideological catalyst in the experience of the conflict in Afghanistan.

In this context, the call to jihad was made in order to confront invasion of a Muslim-majority region by a foreign non-Muslim power. The pivotal thinker in the virulent stream of Islamism that emerged in Afghanistan was a Palestinian,

Abdullah Azzam. While committed to the national liberation of the Palestinian people, Azzam was not of the secular-nationalist hue that defined the Palestinian movement of his time. Instead, his ideological and theological insistence on the shared responsibility to defend Muslim lands under attack from non-Muslim forces took him to Afghanistan. Active throughout the conflict, Azzam headed the Muslim Brotherhood's office in Pakistan and was assassinated in 1989 (Roy 1992:117). Azzam was credited with triggering the transnational nature of the Afghan resistance and his major contribution was the re-identification of jihad as a binding duty for all contemporary Muslims.[13] Azzam asserted, as would the militant Islamists he inspired, that 'jihad and hijra to jihad [migration to enact jihad] have a deep rooted role which cannot be separated from the constitution of [Islam]' (Azzam 2001:25). Similar to Qutb, Azzam identified the decline of Islam as a world power as a result of the ascendance of modernist, non-violent interpretations of jihad.

In the early 1980s, Azzam theorised that the defensive conflict against the Soviet Union was *Fard Kifayah*, a duty from which the majority of Muslims were absolved provided it was discharged by some Muslims (Azzam 2002:19). However, the battle for Afghanistan became entrenched and the Mujahideen proved unable to dispel the Soviet Army quickly. Thus, Azzam reformulated the responsibility of Muslims to assist their brethren in Afghanistan as *Fard Ain*, a binding personal duty applicable to each and every Muslim (Azzam 2001:55). Wiktorowicz (2001:23) asserts that Azzam's perspective held that the duty to repel the invasion of Muslim lands fell initially on those in the immediate vicinity, but in the event of their failure, the required 'geographic proximity for obligatory participation expands', eventually to include the entire *umma*. A similar formulation of the communal responsibility of the Muslim community is present in the doctrines of Hizb al-Tahrir and its splinter organisation al-Muhajiroun (Farouki 1995:49). The Afghan conflict produced many well-known militants who, armed with military experience and indoctrinated in a brutal form of 'Islamic' jihad, scattered throughout the world.

In keeping with the movement's Qutb inspired roots, this loosely affiliated group were often active in 'purging' their own communities of 'infidel' rulers. Oppositional violence in Egypt, Algeria and Central Asia during the 1990s can all be traced back to veterans of Afghanistan. According to Guilain Denoeux (2002:70), two major ideological points define this movement.

> First, their Salafi worldview implies adherence to an orthodox, literalist interpretation of Islam, as well as an implicit or explicit belief in the need for a degree of societal coercion in order to ensure that individuals abide by strict 'Islamic rules.' Second, the violence of the earlier generation of radical Islamists was targeted almost exclusively at the 'unbelieving' ruler, government and

senior officials...of the countries in which these groups operated. That is no longer the case with jihadist Salafis, who have sought to export jihad to new settings, identified new enemies, and tend to see jihad as a global struggle that knows no borders.

The self-perceived success of the Mujahideen in bringing about the withdrawal of the Soviet forces (and even in playing a part in the downfall of the Soviet Union) had spawned a generation of activists committed to a globalised armed struggle.

Azzam's exploration of the role of jihad was clearly influenced by his personal experience of the conflict in Afghanistan. The 'multicultural' reality of the volunteer forces meant finding common ground was important. Thus, the belief in an active physical jihad emerged as a—if not the—major unifying factor for the Mujahideen and the organisations they pioneered. By necessity, a decontextualised reading of jihad became a defining feature of the far-flung militant Islamist movement and was central to the justification of foreign participation in conflicts from Chechnya to the Philippines. As Wiktorowicz (2001:26) points out, 'Azzam's original call to defend the Muslim community in Afghanistan was adopted to extend the jihad indefinitely, moving nomadic jihad into new countries to face infidel oppression'. The Islamist understanding of jihad after Afghanistan was expansive. In Roy's words, jihad increasingly knew 'no political space, no state. Its space is that of the umma' (Roy 1992:154). The demise of the bi-polar system, coupled with the nebulous role of American intelligence agencies in Afghanistan, saw this movement increasingly come to identify the United States as its primary enemy. Thus, the focus of militant Islamism changed from the mid-century preoccupation with the local power structures of the Muslim world to a fixation with the role of the world's only remaining super-power.

Extrapolating from this point, it is evident that thinkers such as Azzam would consider the contemporary conflicts in both Afghanistan and Iraq as *Fard Ain* and therefore posit resistance as a binding individual duty. The challenge posed by the doctrine of jihad in the climate of the 'war on terror' is emphasised by Wiktorowicz (2003:84), who points out that the US-led invasion of Iraq occasioned an endorsement of defensive jihad by the famed Al-Azhar University in Cairo. From the theological and juridical standpoint, the invasion and occupation of Muslim-majority lands by non-Muslim forces fulfils the requirements for defensive action. As Wiktorowicz (2003:84) suggests, while the scholars of Cairo no doubt utilised the term in the context of the 'greater' jihad of non-violent struggle, the legitimacy of a call to defensive 'jihad' in the face of non-Muslim invasions was, by this ruling, theologically affirmed. This reveals the challenging nature of this concept in contemporary Islamic politics.

Significant differences exist over the appropriate methodology (classical or modernist) by which the notion of jihad, *as a defence of Muslim lives and land*, should be undertaken. However, as shown by the Cairo ruling, there is also widespread endorsement of jihad as a *concept* in the name of Islam. This may well link into cross-cultural understandings of the right to self-defence. Politically unpalatable as it may be to a Western audience, the theological (and one could argue political) preconditions for a call to defensive jihad may well have been met by the situation in the Middle East during the 20th century and in the current day. It is the appropriate methodology of the response that poses challenging questions for Muslims, Islamists and the West.

It has been seen that the Islamist worldview draws on a selective mix of the traditional delineations of jihad and fires the passions of its adherents through a focus on political events in the Muslim world. The proponents of contemporary militant Islamism expanded their interpretation of the duty to defend Muslim lands into a program of global attack against their perceived enemies. This movement's call to global jihad, constructed as a physical response to occupation and intervention in the Muslim world, became largely reflexive.

Armed jihad has thus become the defining characteristic of contemporary militant Islamism. Since the Afghan conflict, jihad has become both the means and the end for militant Islamism, as the movement has often failed to articulate a political agenda beyond violence. This has been further complicated by the diverse array of locations in which this movement now operates. In the Muslim world, militant Islamists enact jihad against other Muslims (usually leaders) who are perceived as having 'failed' to uphold the Islamist interpretation of 'Islamic' standards. As has been explored here, such action is a historical feature of this movement. In the international context, jihad is directed at the power structures of the West, especially the United States and its allies.

Conclusion

The emergence of an Islamist movement outside the historical and cultural milieu of the Muslim world is an important development. The attraction of a minority of young Muslims, often Western-born, to Islamism requires exploration. As Roy (2005:360) suggests, the appeal of militant Islamism for young European Muslims is multifaceted:

> Explanations based on poverty, exclusion, racism, acculturation, and so forth may contain kernels of truth, but they are not specific enough to be of much practical help...frustration is obviously a key element in their radicalization, but it seems to have more to do with a particular psychological dimension than with a social or economic one.

The influence of the psychological dimension is further underscored as contemporary Islamism often appears to lack a meaningful and consistent political agenda, especially in the context of non-Muslim arenas such as Europe. Indeed, in the 1990s, Roy (1991:198) presented Islamism in the West as a response, not to colonialism or military invasion, but to the experience of acculturation. Juan Jose Escobar Stemmann (2006) suggests that the appeal of Islamism for Western Muslims, especially in the second and third generations, is based on a similar premise, 'identity problems lead these young people to the path of jihad, where they find respect, brotherhood and a new identity'. Among scholars, this interpretation of Western Islamism as partly a response to the experience of life in Europe *itself* is emerging as an important discourse. This underscores the salience and transferability of Islamist perspectives. This process of globalising Islamism is greatly aided by the minimisation of jurisprudential tradition and by the replacement focus on the need to confront perceived enemies of the faith.

As history progressed, the militant anti-occupation element of the Islamism of the 1980s was reinvigorated and reinforced by the experience of the global 'war on terror'. It could be argued that the contemporary Islamist movement lacks many things: broad-based acceptance within the Muslim world, organisational structure, a clear political strategy and a clear sense of its own revolutionary socio-political potential. Consequently, it has been forced to fall back on simplistic, unifying elements such as violence, especially violence against the West. In essence, Islamism has become more about what its adherents reject than what they actually want. This reactive and simplistic agenda of rejectionism has struck a chord with a minority of Western Muslims. In the contemporary Islamist movement, it could be argued that both theological legitimacy and a sense of a revolutionary societal agenda are lacking. Instead, modern militant Islamism appears informed by a loose interpretation of the inherently politicised worldview of Qutb, with a tendency to resort to slogans and rhetoric regarding the 'revolutionary power of Islam'. This is in contrast to the Islamism of the revival period in which proponents attempted to offer a political doctrine based on Islam which could meaningfully organise and govern society.

The transference of this movement to the United Kingdom was aided by the mid-1990s arrival of preachers influenced by, or personally involved in, the war in Afghanistan. This handful of individuals offered a divisive interpretation of Islam that was significantly removed from the predominately quietist South Asian traditions that had framed the British Muslim community until this time. The Islamist interpretation that flowed from the Afghan experience was largely de-contextualised, highly militant and often committed to a violent application of a specific interpretation of Islam.

This worldview held very limited appeal, but it did strike a chord in marginal sections of the second and third generation British Muslim community. The presentation of an Islam divorced from cultural contexts appealed to the subset of young British Muslims who had little sense of identification with their parents' cultural traditions and, simultaneously, a sense of exclusion from British society. Modood (2006: 48) asserts that 'Islamism [can] offer an alternative source of political mobilisation to egalitarian multiculturalism, or perhaps a complementary one with the former focused on the international and the latter on the national'. This sense of global political mobilisation was reflected and reinforced in the worldview of some of the dissident Arab preachers who arrived in the United Kingdom in the mid-1990s, most notably Omar Bakri Muhammad, Omar Uthman Abu Omar (better known as Sheikh Qatada) and Mustafa Kamel Mustafa (Abu Hamza). The contribution of these three men and their interlinked perspectives on Islam, its relationship with the West and the global Islamist movement were critical to the emergence of Islamism in the United Kingdom.

Notes

1 Muhammad al-Ghazali, a scholar writing in the 1980s, faced a Saudi-led campaign of intimidation after publishing his critique of the Wahhabi influence on Salafism.
2 The Muslim Brotherhood was also active in Jordan in this period. However, the MB hierarchy ensured that the organisation's doctrine was not presented as a challenge to the legitimacy of the state. In effect, the MB functioned as a 'loyal opposition' group in this period, thus having a less tortuous relationship to the authorities (see Wiktorowicz 1999:13).
3 Sheikh Muhammad Omar Bakri of al-Muhajiroun has stated that the organisation's expansion was the result of Nabhani's marriage to a woman from a wealthy Lebanese family that funded his regional political aspirations (see Abedin 2004).
4 This claim has been made by Bakri of al-Muhajiroun (see Abedin 2004).
5 For a strident analysis on the potential threat of Hizb al-Tahrir in Central Asia see Cohen (2003).
6 www.hizb-ut-tahrir.org/EN/, accessed 10 March 2005.
7 www.hizb-ut-tahrir.org//EN/, accessed 10 March 2005.
8 Taqi al-Din Ahmad Ibn Taymiyya, quoted in Peters (1996:47).
9 Ataturk, 1927, quoted in Sayyid (2003:59).
10 'There is no compulsion in religion' (Qur'an 2:256).
11 'The soil of the homeland has, in itself, no value or weight' (see Qutb 1978:130).
12 This document has also been called the creed of Sadat's assassins, as Islamic Jihad the organisation responsible for the assassination of Sadat in 1981 left this leaflet at the scene. It has been translated in full in Jansen (1986).
13 This perhaps explains the Australian government's concern over Azzam's publications. On 11 July 2006, two Azzam texts, *Join the caravan* and *Defense of the Muslim lands*, were banned on the grounds of incitement to terrorism by the Classification Review Board after an application by the Howard government (see Corey 2006).

part three

Al-Muhajiroun

Omar Bakri Muhammad and al-Muhajiroun

In the mid-1990s, the Islamist perspective was gaining strength throughout the Muslim world. Having explored the Salafi movement and the Muslim experience of the late-20th century in Britain it is now possible to situate Islamism, as it emerged in the United Kingdom, within its societal and political context. The aim of this section is to explore how one organisation utilised the Islamist tradition to justify its perspective and actions. One individual's experience is intimately entwined with the evolution of Hizb al-Tahrir in the West and the eventual emergence of al-Muhajiroun. Omar Bakri Muhammad is a name closely associated with Islamism in the United Kingdom. A tabloid favorite during his time in the United Kingdom, Bakri's media presence outstripped his influence and is perhaps indicative of a media and public tendency to need to locate figures to personify political perspectives, especially those political perspectives viewed as confrontational. Most of the information regarding Bakri's life can be traced back to a handful of key media reports and interviews. The most detailed account is Maham Abedin's 2004 article, 'Al-Muhajiroun in the United Kingdom: an interview with Sheikh Omar Bakri Muhammad' which was published in several locations and upon the website www.muhajiroun.com. This version of Bakri's personal history is confirmed by the well-respected scholar Quintain Wiktorowicz who conducted a series of interviews with Bakri in London during 2002. However, in a July 2007 interview with the author, Bakri denied the commonly-held version of his life, instead claiming a significantly different personal history. Bakri rejected the Abedin article in its totality, claiming he 'bluffed' the interviewer who was, according to Bakri, determined to discredit him (Bakri 2007). Bakri alleges that he allowed the prevailing version of his history to be publicly disseminated to demonstrate to his followers the untrustworthiness of the mainstream media (Bakri 2007). The new situation in which Bakri finds himself, essentially exiled in Tripoli, Lebanon and separated from his wife and family, may well have contributed significantly to this re-orientation, even softening, of his personal history. In the interest of providing an exhaustive account, the above mentioned version of Bakri's personal history, as explained in mid-2007, is also recounted here.

The commonly-held version of Bakri's life tells a story of a classic Islamist awakening, with participation in major organisations and the near-mandatory tales of activism and deportation. In this version, Omar Bakri Muhammad was born in Syria in 1958, allegedly to a wealthy family from Aleppo (Faramarzi 2005). Bakri's political activism was expressed in an Islamic framework from early in life and he joined the Muslim Brotherhood as a teenager. The Muslim Brotherhood was committed to agitation against the secular-nationalist rule of Syrian President Hafez Assad, whose embrace of secularism and alliance with the Soviet Union had drawn significant criticism from some circles. Bakri was expelled from Syria in one of the Ba'thist government's numerous crackdowns on the Muslim Brotherhood. The rationale behind Bakri's subsequent decision to leave the Muslim Brotherhood is unclear but after moving to Lebanon in the late 1970s he joined the banned Hizb al-Tahrir. It can be speculated that Bakri's attraction to Hizb al-Tahrir was the organisation's more expansive worldview. The Muslim Brotherhood, while a regional organisation, often focused its action on the individual state level in line with its doctrine of Islamisation through education and grassroots activism. By contrast Hizb al-Tahrir was firmly committed to the restoration of the Caliphate, a much more dramatic objective. Bakri's education in Islamic history, politics and culture may have been undertaken in some of the region's most famed academic institutions, such as Cairo's Al-Azhar University, but it was sporadic. Disputes with academic staff saw Bakri depart Cairo and enrol at The Islamic School of al-Saltiyah in Mecca, Saudi Arabia. This appears to have been a major turning point in the young activist's life as after years of indoctrination in the tenets of political Islam, Bakri sought to develop his own profile within Islamist circles.

Hizb al-Tahrir, with its doctrine of pan-Islamism, was banned in the conservative Kingdom of Saudi Arabia. The Saudi Royals, committed to their own Wahhabi interpretation of Islam, controlled the Kingdom with repressive force. The geographic location of Saudi Arabia, the birthplace of Islam, has historically lent authority to the state's leadership aspirations in the Muslim world. Conversely, it has opened the ruling hierarchy to frequent challenges as organisations and individuals draw inspiration from a location that is embedded with Islamic meaning. It appears Bakri decided to follow this course. Hizb al-Tahrir had a presence in neighbouring Kuwait and Bakri drew support from the Kuwaiti branch as he attempted to organise a cell in Saudi Arabia. Bakri has claimed he enjoyed a limited success in this mission, creating a group of 39 men who subscribed to the Hizb al-Tahrir vision (Abedin 2004). In a move that foretold the future disintegration of relations between Bakri and Hizb al-Tahrir, the regional leadership suspended Bakri's membership. Even at this young age, it appears that Bakri's renegade agenda raised concerns within the traditionally secretive organisation. Bakri did not, however, abandon his Islamist agenda as a result of this setback. Perhaps inspired by his Saudi Arabian location and its place within Islamic history, Bakri chose a symbolic date, 2 March 1983, the anniversary of the dissolution of the Caliphate, to launch his own organisation, al-Muhajiroun (Abedin 2004). As is the case with many aspects of Bakri's life this is contested. Wiktorowicz presents a slightly different account, suggesting the new organisation was not formally launched. Instead it announced its existence through the publication of leaflets challenging the Royal Family's right to rule (Wiktorowicz 2005). According to Wiktorowicz's text, Bakri was then arrested, interrogated and deported along with six others (Wiktorowicz 2005). The charge upon which Bakri's deportation from the Kingdom rested was teaching from a range of Hizb al-Tahrir texts. This allowed authorities to link him to the banned party. It also suggests that despite Bakri's departure from Hizb al Tahrir, his ideological and intellectual perspective was still closely aligned to that of his former party.

In the Qur'an the Prophet's journey from Mecca to Medina signals an important turning point in the life of the early Muslim community. In the modern era, the notion of emigration has often played a politically and theologically-charged role. The concept has often been utilised by Islamists who call for the faithful to remove themselves from the temptations and failings of the community at large. For example, Qutb asserted that *hijra* from the *jahili* society is needed in order for the revolutionary vanguard to remain focused on the task of societal transformation (Bonney 2004:222). Bakri named his organisation 'the Emigrants' in an attempt to draw on this strain of historical consciousness. Bakri, expelled from Saudi Arabia, found himself on the move once again. In early 1986, he applied for visas to Malaysia and Pakistan, both populous Muslim countries. Bakri arrived in London to await the outcomes of these applications and was apparently offered an olive branch by the European wing of Hizb al-Tahrir. He returned to the organisation and subsequently remained in London, building a Hizb al-Tahrir party structure in the United Kingdom (Abedin 2004). This was an important development as it was Bakri's first attempt at a political organisation outside the Muslim world. A succession of businesses was then opened to finance the movement's activities and Bakri committed significant time and resources to the development of Hizb al-Tahrir in the United Kingdom.

In 2007, this version of his history was contested by Bakri who claims he was born in Lebanon and was slated by his family to become an Islamic scholar.

He also denies any involvement in or membership of the Muslim Brotherhood (Bakri 2007). Linked to this point, Bakri now rejects any involvement in political agitation in Syria and claims to have left Lebanon for Saudi Arabia as a result of the havoc wreaked by the Lebanese civil war (Bakri 2007). During his time in Saudi Arabia, Bakri claims he worked as a manager of a major electricity company. He also continued his study of Islam. The conventional version of al-Muhajiroun's history holds that the group was formed in Saudi Arabia as an offshoot of Hizb al-Tahrir. Bakri acknowledges the 'seed of an organisation' existed in the study circles he created, but refutes the claim an organisation was formed in this period (Bakri 2007). Bakri also contends he left Saudi Arabia voluntarily and was on good terms with the authorities there. This differs markedly from the established version of Bakri's life. As the situation in Lebanon remained unstable, Bakri claims he moved to the United Kingdom where he was granted indefinite leave to remain. Bakri asserts that it is *haram* for Muslims to remain among non-Muslims unless the conditions enable the practice of the faith and room to enact *da'wa*. As the United Kingdom met these requirements, Bakri made the decision to stay.

Once in the United Kingdom, Bakri contends that he established the al-Khilafa movement as a result of the Islamic traditions encouraging Muslims to organise for the benefit of the community. Bakri claims this organisation had a membership of about 100 people when he was approached by Hizb al-Tahrir. In this interpretation, which privileges Bakri's personal role, he literally suggests that Hizb al-Tahrir 'joined him' (Bakri 2007). As a result of the shared focus on the need to re-establish an Islamic state, Bakri merged with the floundering Hizb al-Tahrir. Bakri attributes the resurgence of Hizb al-Tahrir in the 1990s largely to his leadership (Bakri 2007).

The contested nature of his life before the United Kingdom aside, Bakri clearly found himself operating in a state that offered much greater space to articulate dissent than had been the case in the Arab countries of his youth. The United Kingdom's traditionally open society and determination to uphold the liberal-democratic concept of freedom of speech offered Bakri a new platform: the media. Bakri sprung to prominence during the 1991 Gulf War with his assertion that, if travelling in a Muslim majority country, then-Prime Minister John Major would be a legitimate target for assassination (*British Muslims* 2001a:1). Bakri continually stepped up his rhetoric, perhaps emboldened by the novel experience of articulating such statements against the authorities in his state of residence without consequence. This determination to secure a media presence led Bakri back into a direct confrontation with the leadership hierarchy of Hizb al-Tahrir. Bakri's desire to develop a media presence was coupled with his increasing propensity to comment on situations specific to the British Muslim community. Hizb al-Tahrir, while often emerging within states in response to local disillusionment and issues, was a strongly anti-nationalist organisation. Bakri challenged this focus with his on-going rhetoric on the experiences of a specific group of Muslims, moreover a specific group of Muslims residing outside *dar al-Islam*. This was perhaps identified as contradictory to the focus and direction of Hizb al-Tahrir, a perception that may well have been compounded by Bakri's increasing willingness to call for the restoration of the Caliphate, *outside* the Muslim world. To the frustration of both Hizb al-Tahrir and the mainstream British Muslim community, Bakri began to assert that the restoration of the Caliphate can and should begin wherever Muslims live, including in the United Kingdom. Bakri's shift to this position may well have been a result of the relative freedom he had been accorded by the British state in the propagation of his Islamist perspectives. It also marked his organisation as different within international Islamism. According to Ayoob, the willingness to focus on the restoration of the Caliphate differentiated Hizb al-Tahrir, and thus by extension al-Muhajiroun, from the broader Islamist movement that had internalised the doctrine of state-based nationalism in the Muslim world (Ayoob 2005).

Bakri's new found premise, that Western states with their willingness to allow the expression of dissent were the best places in which to agitate for a global Islamic revolution, proved dangerous and divisive to the established British Muslim community. Simultaneously, such controversial and nearly facetious calls guaranteed Bakri a greater media profile. Eventually, the Hizb al-Tahrir leadership could no longer tolerate Bakri's determination to seek an individual profile and he parted ways with the organisation once again. Bakri walked a difficult line, as a product of a Hizb al-Tahrir education he was well-versed on the importance of radical renewal and the restoration of the Caliphate as the panacea of the Muslim condition. However, in this phase of his life Bakri found himself in London, facing new pressures and opportunities that required some intellectual and theological innovations. While the British system allowed greater freedom of expression than Bakri was accustomed to, his desire to remain in the United Kingdom dictated that some restraint and caution was required. Bakri thus focused on the division of the global Muslim responsibility. Throughout his time in the United Kingdom, Bakri drew distinctions regarding the responsibilities of Muslims in the Muslim world and those in the West. However, at the core of Bakri's worldview was the assertion of incompatibility between Islam and Western norms such as secularism

Considering this deeply politicised worldview, and his new-found media presence, Bakri's departure from Hizb al-Tahrir did not signal the end of his tenure in the public eye. Bakri relaunched the dormant al-Muhajiroun in the mid-1990s and simultaneously morphed from a renegade spokesman for a secretive global organisation into the very public leader of a distinct group. At the time, Bakri asserted theological differences existed. However, remembering his alleged use of Hizb al-Tahrir texts in Saudi Arabia during his previous hiatus from the party, this claim seems questionable. It has been suggested that the cleaving point between Bakri and Hizb al-Tahrir had little to do with doctrine and more to do with power. As Suha Taji Farouki opines, under pressure to conform to the expectation of the party's leadership, Bakri 'evidently decided he would rather quit than relinquish the political leadership and popular public momentum he had successfully developed' (Farouki 2000:31). Now an autonomous actor on the British Islamist scene Bakri continued to develop his public profile.

In 2007, Bakri presents his departure from Hizb al-Tahrir as the result of tensions which had begun to surface between the international leadership, based in Jordan, and Bakri's London-based wing (Bakri 2007). Specifically, he claims theological differences and the publication of jurisprudential rulings which 'contradicted Islam' led to his decision to leave the organisation (Bakri 2007). He resigned from Hizb al-Tahrir on 15 January 1996 and announced the presence of al-Muhajiroun three days later. Bakri claims it was this decision, to re-organise politically (and thus in direct competition), which soured his relationship with Hizb al-Tahrir. Ideologically, Bakri has argued that Hizb al-Tahrir's Arab-centric focus was problematic given the organisation's predominately South Asian support base in the United Kingdom. The rationale aside, Bakri's decision to leave Hizb al-Tahrir clearly signalled a new phase in his Islamist career. Wiktorowicz is in agreement with Bakri that the establishment of al-Muhajiroun 'sent shockwaves through the global [Hizb al-Tahrir] movement' (Wiktorowicz 2005). Many disaffected Hizb al-Tahrir supporters sought to join al-Muhajiroun. They were attracted by the new focus on public activism and agitation which, in contrast to Hizb al-Tahrir, Bakri argued should occur wherever Muslims resided. In this way, Bakri claims he was determined to put 'the ideology above the group' (Bakri 2007). Moreover, Bakri was joined in London by some students from his Saudi days and from amongst this circle and the ex-Hizb al-Tahrir followers he selected a 'new core, the second generation' (Bakri 2007). These individuals became the basis of al-Muhajiroun. Many of these men were lawyers, meaning Bakri had access to a skill-set which assisted him to 'be on the edge, but stay within the law' (Bakri 2007). Given Bakri's media presence and his industrious pursuit of a public profile for his new organisation these skills were sorely needed. Bakri continually tried to draw links between the experiences of Muslims in Britain and those in conflict scenarios in the Muslim world. The pro-active aspect of Bakri's worldview was the assertion that a restoration of the Caliphate would provide political salvation and succour for Muslims globally.

Yet solutions proved ineffective as sound bites, thus Bakri's focus was usually upon the perceived problem: either the British state (domestically) or Western and particularly American foreign policy (internationally). In its rhetoric on the experience of Muslims in the Middle East, al-Muhajiroun followed a two-pronged approach. Firstly, the role of the West was condemned. Secondly, the rule of contemporary Arab/Muslim leaders was rejected. The response to these issues was presented as jihad to establish Sharia and the eventual restoration of the Caliphate in a global format. This clearly reflects the legacy of Hizb al-Tahrir.

In its perspectives on Arab/Muslim state-based leaders al-Muhajiroun clearly honoured the legacy of Sayyid Qutb. Arab leaders from Palestine to Saudi Arabia were condemned as Western puppets, serving the United States above the needs of their people (Al-Muhajiroun 2002b). While Bakri's media profile rose, the organisation he headed never moved beyond a marginal status. Al-Muhajiroun attempted to attract membership from a Muslim generation that Felice Dassetto (2003:507) contends has experienced a 'process of socialization towards radical Islamism'. This generation was born between 1970 and 1985 and its political consciousness developed in an era marked by influences such as the conflict in Afghanistan, the Rushdie affair, the 1991 Gulf War and the ever-present question of Palestine. Prior to the events of 11 September 2001, al-Muhajiroun had little success in creating a strong public profile. The organisation was further restricted by the presence of its parent body. Hizb al-Tahrir remained committed to its own program and retained significant levels of support. Al-Muhajiroun's appeal was limited to young, disillusioned Muslims and most scholarly opinion places the group's total membership at only a few hundred. However, Bakri regularly preached to a much wider audience, either via the media or in latter years, the internet. The very public and controversial profile sought by Bakri was widely condemned in Hizb al-Tahrir circles.

The British response to al-Muhajiroun in this period can best be described as dismissive bemusement. However, over time, the real challenge posed by al-Muhajiroun was one of affiliation. The potential of al-Muhajiroun to act as a conduit to more dangerous international organisations was publicly flagged on numerous occasions. Bakri, by now settled in the United Kingdom, applied for citizenship on three occasions. However, his public profile and the difficulties associated with acting against an individual with citizenship led cautious authorities to deny his applications. In addition to his role as the grand Amir of al-Muhajiroun, Bakri founded the Al-Khilafa publishing house, which published most of the Hizb al-Tahrir texts in the United Kingdom. Again, the interplay between Hizb al-Tahrir and the offshoot of al-Muhajiroun requires consideration.

Bakri also engaged with the legalistic traditions of Islam, teaching at the Sharia College and serving on the United Kingdom Sharia Court.

Al-Muhajiroun, until 2001, was largely confined to the shadows of the British Muslim political scene, its divisive and inflammatory rhetoric holding little attraction for those it attempted to influence. However, the attacks of 11 September 2001 propelled the organisation into the media spotlight. Following the terrorist attacks, al-Muhajiroun identified itself as aligned to international Islamism, repeatedly endorsing the ideology of Osama bin Laden and al-Qaeda.

> We will continue to support the sincere scholars, activists and Mujahideen, such as Sheikh Usama bin Laden, as long as their word and sword are risen for the dignity of Islam, as long as their terror is targeted against the enemy of Allah and as long as their effort is to preserve the dignity of the Muslims after the apostate rulers have lost it (Al-Muhajiroun 2003c).

For al-Muhajiroun, it appears bin Laden provided the perfect inspiration and he was continually lauded by the organisation as part of the attempt to situate itself as a voice of Islamism in the West.

Al-Muhajiroun claimed a limited membership throughout the United Kingdom and a presence in the United States, Pakistan, Lebanon and France. In March 2004, the Pakistani branch ceded from the main organisation apparently in order to participate more actively in the militant Islamist activity in Afghanistan. According to American sources, al-Muhajiroun Pakistan (which dropped the al-Muhajiroun title after the succession) then 'evolved into one of many support networks connecting Western Muslim youths, mostly from Europe, to the jihadist theatre in Southwest Asia. Bakri blessed this decision; clearly, he wanted to maintain plausible deniability for the group as a whole' (WTR 2006).

Theoretically al-Muhajiroun drew on the Salafi tradition. As Bakri moved closer to a Salafist mindset this influence became more evident. Using Oliver Roy's categorisations al-Muhajiroun could also be identified as 'neo-fundamentalist' (Roy 2004). According to Bubalo and Fealy, neo-fundamentalists 'bypass the nation-state and focus on individual Muslims and on a supranational, if largely virtual *umma*. Unsurprisingly, it has been largely the uprooted and the dislocated who have drifted toward neo-fundamentalism' (Bubalo & Fealy 2005:30). When juxtaposed against Bakri's life history, this passage is pertinent. Al-Muhajiroun consistently focused on the sense of social dislocation and alienation it believed Muslims should feel within the West. From this position, the organisation sought to encourage a stance of absolute rejection of the Western nation-state system among its followers.

Al-Muhajiroun's desire to foster a sense of dislocation was evident in all its public pronouncements. The organisation consistently warned against assimilation, integration and even friendship between Muslims and non-Muslims. Using literal and often de-contextualised segments of the Qur'an, al-Muhajiroun presented an interpretation of Islam in which the utter alienation of Muslims from their non-Muslim surroundings was central. Al-Muhajiroun privileged exclusionary doctrines and asserted that Muslims should avoid all forms of contact with non-Muslims. British attempts at engagement, such as the interfaith movement, were thus rejected as 'a false cursed notion' (Al-Muhajiroun 2003h).

Al-Muhajiroun's determination to drive a wedge between Western Muslims and their states of residence was premised on the assertion that multiculturalism did not mean mutual respect and that beyond the rhetoric of equality Muslims were, and would always be seen as, different.

> So we see that the Kuffar always ask for reparations for their dead, as in Poland and in New York but when it comes to Muslims in Chechnya, Kashmir or Palestine, their lives are seen not to be worth as much. There are no minutes silence, no mourning and no compensation for Muslims. Even animals in the West have more rights than Muslims (Al-Muhajiroun 2003h).

From this premise, al-Muhajiroun argued that Muslims should abandon all attempts at co-existence. It regularly castigated Western Muslim organisations that engaged with the broader discourses of the state. For al-Muhajiroun, Islam could not be adapted to co-exist with secular modes of governance. The organisation thus attempted to isolate and alienate its followers by asserting their difference. It frequently stated that interaction between Muslims and non-Muslims was undesirable, even un-Islamic, asserting that 'to side with the Kuffar against Muslims is considered to be an act of apostasy' (Al-Muhajiroun 2003i). This carried over into the al-Muhajiroun perspective on the rights of Muslims to participate in the functioning of the state.

> Muslims must not vote for anyone in the present election, even if they say that they are going to get you some schools or other benefits for the Muslim community. How can a Muslim say that there is no legislator except Allah (SWT) and then vote for someone else to legislate Kuffar law and order? Rather every Muslim's Tawheed dictates that he keeps Allah (SWT)'s sanctity exclusive, ie to obey, worship and follow him exclusively (Al-Muhajiroun 2004l).

However, al-Muhajiroun did not limit itself to commenting on domestic issues. The understanding of jihad within al-Muhajiroun's rhetoric was militant and global in scope. The rulers of the Arab-Muslim world were usually rejected as apostates. Furthermore, the organisation endorsed violent jihad as the appropriate solution to the ills of the global Muslim community. This de-contextualised message of Islam, characteristic of jihadist Salafism, was employed by al-Muhajiroun as it sought to attract disaffected Muslims to its ranks.

However, the interplay of Wahhabi norms with the Salafi tradition complicates the identification of al-Muhajiroun. Despite the shared Salafi basis many international groups, including al-Muhajiroun, did not support the Royal Family of Saudi Arabia. Despite Bakri's endorsement of Saudi Arabia in 2007, most of al-Muhajiroun's rhetoric called for the Royal Family's overthrow. Al-Muhajiroun's equivocal stance on Wahhabism may stem from Hizb al-Tahrir's conflicted relationship with the Wahhabi movement, a relationship fraught by differences in focus and interpretation of the Qur'an (Naumkin 2005:128). However, al-Muhajiroun's rejection of the Saudi Royals may have a less theological basis. According to the conventional version of his life, Bakri was expelled from the Kingdom for agitation against the Royal Family and this may well explain al-Muhajiroun's determination to present the Saudi system as a 'false' application of the Salafi tradition. However, in a strange distinction, the founder of the nation, Sheikh Muhammad ibn Abdul Wahhab was venerated by al-Muhajiroun as the example that contemporary Mujahideen and martyrs should emulate.

Adherents of the Salafi tradition usually display a tendency to seek reformation within the Islamic world, to shape and affect society and cultural trends within Muslim-dominated nations. A London-based organisation, al-Muhajiroun's innovation was that it sought to Islamise Western society first. According to exhaustive empirical research by Hassan, al-Muhajiroun's central tenet, the need to create a society based on Islamic principles and the Sharia, is a deeply-held belief in the Muslim world. In endorsing this ideal, al-Muhajiroun, like numerous other organisations from across the spectrum of Islamist thought, tapped into a deeply-entrenched current of contemporary Muslim political thought: that secularism has failed and Islamic norms provide the best organisational principle for society.[1] The translation of this belief into a Western state setting was obviously highly problematic. The organisation's perspective on the role of Western Muslims and the relationship between Muslims and non-Muslims was undeniably marginal yet it is this central contention: that the existing structures of governance have failed Muslims everywhere, which emerged as the true challenge if not al-Muhajiroun itself, then the Islamist impulse of which it was a manifestation.

Al-Muhajiroun rejected Western military, political or social intervention in the Muslim world. The organisation devoted a significant proportion of its linked to al-Muhajiroun have included: the Islamic Council of Britain, the Society of Muslim Lawyers, the Shariah Court of the United Kingdom, the Society of Converts to Islam, the International Islamic Front and the Muslim Youth League. The level of autonomy of each these groups was questionable, as Bakri was a self-described judge on the Shariah Court and spokesman for the International Islamic Front, while another important al-Muhajiroun spokesperson, Anjem Choudry, was the President of The Society of Muslim Lawyers.[3] Against this backdrop of affiliations, (which may have presented Bakri in a less marginal light than was deserved) his inflammatory statements led to scores of interviews in a range of media sources. The media's willingness to privilege Bakri's views only gave further impetus and encouragement to his rhetoric. It is not surprising that in the post-September 11 climate Bakri's interpretation of the concept of jihad was one of the major drawcards for a sensationalistic media.

As explored, in the contemporary period mainstream Islam has displayed a tendency to understand jihad in a non-militaristic way. This trend is even more pronounced in Western Muslim communities. While the majority of organisations prefer to emphasise the plethora of religious directives that focus on co-existence and equilibrium, there remains a current of political disillusionment and dissatisfaction that is often framed by the advocacy of militant jihad. For al-Muhajiroun this was important. The primary objective of al-Muhajiroun was the re-establishment of the Caliphate, a result which cannot be achieved while Muslim lands are occupied or ruled by non-Islamic or secular regimes. To al-Muhajiroun, 'Islam has only one answer to…occupation and aggression, and that is Jihad for the cause of Allah' (Al-Muhajiroun 2002a).

Similar to the Qutb and Egyptian Islamic Jihad examples, the organisation rejected modernist interpretations and asserted Islam's universal claim. The al-Muhajiroun understanding of jihad was the use of 'military force, where diplomacy fails, to remove the obstacles the Islamic state faces in carrying its ideology to mankind' (Al-Muhajiroun 2003a). To al-Muhajiroun, there was 'no doubt that fighting the enemy, whether the part which is near to you or that which is far away, is a duty upon Muslims' (Al-Muhajiroun 2003c). In al-Muhajiroun's interpretation jihad was not anti-Christian or anti-US rather it was anti-kafir (McRoy 2005). Thus it could be applied against Muslim leaders perceived as failing in their 'Islamic' duty. This clearly reflects the thought of Qutb on the apostate leader. However, the organisation also drew on the jihadist Salafi tradition and focused its attention on the need for a militaristic jihad to confront Israel, and in the aftermath of the occupation of Iraq, the United States. Militaristic jihad was endorsed by the organisation and seen as a program of political transformation that would succeed where other forms of agitation, such as peaceful mobilisation, had failed.

We see nowadays that there is nothing that shakes the enemy except the attacking and bombing and violence for the sake of Allah. In Palestine, the Jews suffer and feel as if they are in hell because of the regular daily attacks and operations, but they never felt any fear or suffering from demonstrations in London (Al-Muhajiroun 2004c).

In addition to Qutb, al-Muhajiroun's doctrinal perspective on the interlinked issues of jihad and terrorism drew selectively from sources such as Abdullah Azzam and Osama bin Laden. Azzam's view of the responsibility to confront aggression and occupation was endorsed. Yet Azzam had also asserted that the provision of financial assistance did not absolve the individual Muslim from personal involvement if the community under threat proved unable to repel the invading force. This prescription alone ensured that al-Muhajiroun, comfortably ensconced in London, was unlikely to adhere completely to his standards which would have entailed a departure from the United Kingdom (Azzam 2001:51). Therefore, al-Muhajiroun's endorsement of active jihad as a binding duty of universal applicability appeared highly problematic considering its geographical location. Bakri, in a demonstration of his sporadic willingness to read Islam as historically specific, repeatedly rejected the necessity of migration to *dar al-Islam* for Muslims living in the West. Indeed, in 2007, Bakri denied having recruited people for international jihadi activity, arguing it was counter-intuitive that he would send his most committed students overseas when they could be furthering al-Muhajiroun's cause in the United Kingdom (Bakri 2007). In its early years, al-Muhajiroun asserted that jihad was a legitimate form of defence against attack. Then, drawing heavily on Qutb's notion of jihad as a force for removing all obstacles preventing Islam from assuming its position as the global authority structure, the organisation advanced the following interpretation:

Muslims and non-Muslims have misunderstood the concept of Jihad. To non-Muslims, Jihad is presented as the diabolical call of 'blood-thirsty people' to convert others to Islam by 'the sword'. To Muslims, on the other hand, it has been promoted as a self-help concept whose aim is to make one a model citizen in whatever society he finds himself in. Neither of these ideas represent [*sic*] the reality of Jihad...At best, its legal meaning can be understood as 'using military force, where diplomacy fails, to remove the obstacles the Islamic State faces in carrying its ideology to mankind' (Al-Muhajiroun 2004m).

As this passage indicates, al-Muhajiroun explicitly rejected the notion of the 'greater' or non-physical jihad that is prevalent in the modernist tradition. Al-Muhajiroun sought to legitimise jihad as a collective, physical response of the Muslim community. By linking the idea of jihad to that of 'foreign policy', al-Muhajiroun attempted to draw on familiar Western notions of state action and authority. Considering the organisation's underlying belief in the need for a pan-Islamic state, this approach makes sense. It is, however, also an attempt to side-step the reality that no such state exists. This interpretation, which (problematically) assumes the unity of the Muslim world, appears to understand the *umma* as acting in lieu of a unified Islamic state and asserts the legitimacy of the defensive jihad in the contemporary political context. As explored, the Islamic requirement of aiding Muslims under attack is also premised on the inviolability of the *umma* and the responsibility of the individual Muslim to defend it. Azzam took this position to the extreme and declared physical jihad the legitimate and binding response. In a global climate partly characterised by invasion and occupation of Muslim lands and the consequent suffering of Muslim civilians, this mindset is potentially attractive.

Despite residing in the heart of the 'enemy', al-Muhajiroun did not call on its followers to attack the British State (Al-Muhajiroun 2003e). The organisation instead divided jihad into a range of duties dependent on the individual's circumstances and location, citing that 'each and every Muslim must contribute verbally, physically and financially,' dependant on their means (Al-Muhajiroun 2003c). Within the United Kingdom, al-Muhajiroun saw itself as a 'fifth column' (Al-Muhajiroun 2003f), preparing to support the resurgent Caliphate. By early 2005, Bakri was reported as asserting that all non-believers were legitimate targets of jihad, as 'complicity in the acts of one's rulers make one a legitimate target' (McRoy 2005). This can be interpreted as justifying attacks upon the civilian populations of America and Britain in the context of their governments' prosecution of the 'war on terror'. Even from an al-Muhajiroun style position, which condones jihad, this was—or should have been—deeply problematic in the context of democratic societies, where a proportion of the population, sometimes a significant proportion, may be fervently opposed to existing policies.

In line with the development of Islamist theory, al-Muhajiroun understood jihad as an individual duty and drew on the traditional defensive/offensive division. Historically, the Sunni modernist position has been that without a Caliph's authorisation no legitimate offensive jihad can be undertaken (Johnson 1997:128). In a post-Caliphate period this position essentially forbids jihad. Today, with Muslim lands diminished and in some cases under foreign occupation, the offensive/defensive split becomes more problematic. The challenge of the jihad doctrine is not the offensive category (although in Qutb's conception the lack of legitimate authority does not appear to be an obstacle) but the defensive understanding of jihad. In the context of Western-led invasions of various Muslim lands the defensive understanding of jihad appears to dovetail with current affairs (Batley 2003:7). The contemporary period, manifestly different from the social and political climate in which this doctrine was formulated, has seen a blending of the concepts of offensive and defensive action. For organisations such as al-Muhajiroun, this was a recruitment coup.

However, in line with the legacy of Qutb, al-Muhajiroun did not restrict itself to advocacy of the defensive jihad. Instead it blurred defensive and offensive understandings in the paradigm of Islam's universal claim.

> [Do] not make the operations reactionary but rather a continuous assault on the enemies without giving them time to breath. The battlefield must not have any borders or nationality. The enemy is all over the world so we need to fight them wherever we meet them. We must revive the mentality of jihad and the mentality to fight against the enemy (Al-Muhajiroun 2004e).

This understanding, clearly militaristic, repositioned expansionist jihad as a central tenet of the Islamic identity and the Islamic community. Al-Muhajiroun clearly adhered to the notion of absolute or static divisions between Muslims and the West. Citing Osama bin Laden as the authority, al-Muhajiroun claimed the world had been divided into two camps 'the camp of Islam and the camp of kuffar' and presented the duty of the 'camp of Islam' as to expand and conquer the 'camp of kuffar' (Al-Muhajiroun 2004d). Such statements reflect al-Muhajiroun's acceptance of the Islamic equivalent of Huntington's 'clash of civilisations' thesis, the *dar al-harb* and *dar al-islam* (abode of war and abode of peace) delineation.[4] This deeply confrontational worldview informed every aspect of al-Muhajiroun's rhetoric. As Khaled Abdou El Fadl points out, this understanding of the world, popular among most contemporary Islamist organisations, is not Qur'anic. In the text 'Muslims are a single nation before God, but (the Qur'an) does not bifurcate the world into two or more abodes' (El Fadl 2005:230).

Al-Muhajiroun understood the Western Muslim responsibility was to remain in the West and strengthen Muslim communities in preparation for the return of the Caliphate. In reality, the reason was no doubt more pragmatic. Al-Muhajiroun, with its radical rejection of the nation-state and its criticism of existing leadership, would have faced severe persecution in the Muslim world. The historical experience of Hizb al-Tahrir confirms this. Freedom of expression, a characteristic of liberal democracies, gave al-Muhajiroun the social and political space to disseminate its anti-Western perspectives. Despite this, al-Muhajiroun strongly rejected the integration of Western Muslims into their societies. In the attempt to arrest this process, al-Muhajiroun consistently strove to contrast Western society with Islam, in its reading a de-contextualised and often idealised system.

> A brief glimpse at any western society, like the USA and UK, run on values of freedom, secularism and democracy will reveal a complete breakdown in the social and moral fabric with homosexuality, paedophilia, adultery, promiscuity, fornication, pornography and abortion rampant, not forgetting all the sexually transmitted diseases that come hand in hand with such liberalism. All of this exposes gross incompetence on the part of those ruling in looking after the welfare

of the masses, in providing for their basic needs and in protecting the citizens from exploitation of their emotions and desires, leading to diseases, depression and uncontrollable crime reflected in the statistics for murders, thefts, suicides and rapes in the West (Al-Muhajiroun 2002c).

In order to prevent the integration of Muslims in the West, al-Muhajiroun strove to focus Muslim attention elsewhere. Reflecting elements of the Islamist tradition distilled by Azzam, al-Muhajiroun consistently asserted it was the responsibility of Muslims to assist their fellow Muslims in conflict zones by any and all means. The war in Afghanistan led to significant public debate in the United Kingdom and al-Muhajiroun appeared determined to be involved. Accused of recruiting British Muslims to fight alongside the Taliban and al-Qaeda, Bakri achieved greater public prominence by his pronouncement of Prime Minister Tony Blair as a legitimate target after the invasion of Afghanistan (*British Muslims* 2001d:3). Considering the development of the 'war on terror', al-Muhajiroun was constantly provided opportunities to extend its rhetoric.[5] As Western forces entered Afghanistan and then Iraq, the perception that the 'war on terror' was in reality a 'war on Islam' grew. In this situation, the relationship between British Muslims and the state gained an ever greater importance. Al-Muhajiroun was particularly scathing of Muslims who participated in the organs of state security. The irony of this position was underscored by Bakri's personal circumstances. In 1996, Bakri's period of financial independence had come to an end and for the remainder of his time in the United Kingdom he was a recipient of financial assistance from the state, a reality which, when it became public, triggered the need for some fancy theological and theoretical footwork. In a clear example of the kind of equivocation which raised the ire of the British public, Bakri asserted that it was permissible to 'benefit from democracy but give it no legitimacy' (Bakri 2007). Bakri's tendency to 'pick and choose' was a feature of his time in the United Kingdom. Bakri finds no inconsistency in his actions, basically suggesting the system exists to be exploited. However, his willingness to accept some elements of the British system, while rejecting others, was highly problematic and gave weighty legitimacy to the campaign against him.

The need to view al-Muhajiroun within the broader socio-political context in which it operated is important here, as such debates gained greater importance with the continuation of the 'war on terror'. For example, al-Muhajiroun consistently condemned the participation of Muslims in the police force or security agencies. This correlates with Bakri's overall rejection of Muslims allying themselves within non-Muslims. Again, the flexibility of such positions was made clear in 2007 when Bakri clarified, or potentially moderated, this view. Rather than a blanket assertion that Muslims who joined the British army were committing apostasy, which was the dominant perspective in al-Muhajiroun's literature, Bakri presented this as the lesser transgression of a sin (Bakri 2007). To Bakri, this action only becomes an act of apostasy if the Muslim serves in a Muslim-majority region, so essentially if the British Muslim participates in military action against other Muslims. In some ways, this is merely an extension of the overarching assertion that Muslims must affirm their loyalty to the *umma* over their state of residence. However, Bakri is quick to reinforce his underlying interpretation of the relationship between Muslims and non-Muslims, suggesting from a national security perspective, Western states should prevent Muslims joining the army, in case they 'change their mind' (Bakri 2007). Again, the determination to differentiate and drive a wedge between British Muslims and their fellow citizens is clear. Overall, Bakri claims Muslims should live in the West and interact with non-Muslims, but that they should not integrate, 'expect the same position' as locally-born citizens or participate in the security of the state (Bakri 2007). In this way, Bakri presents patriotism as a notion which only people born into a national community can feel and, thus, seeks to undermine the entire basis of Western multiculturalism which in essence affirms the opposite.

Internationally, al-Muhajiroun focused on the need for violence as a political response to the reality of non-Muslim occupation of Muslim lands. This was one of the starkest points of contrast between the al-Muhajiroun position and that of mainstream British Muslims, many of whom (in common with many non-Muslim Britons) also rejected their state's foreign policy. As the 'war on terror' dissolved in the blood-letting that engulfed 'liberated' Iraq, the al-Muhajiroun position hardened, with terrorism endorsed in any and all forms. This eventually included statements of support, if not outright glorification, of suicide bombings against civilian targets. Al-Muhajiroun (2004c) asserted 'there is no doubt that bombing the Kuffar in Muslim lands and the lands of the Kuffar will terrify them, anger them and deter them from attacking us again'. Muslim rejection of terrorism and violence was met with derision by the organisation.

> Without any doubt, terrorism against them [the USA] is obligatory...The Muslims readily attack and condemn other Muslims because they commit terrorist acts, yet they do not know that Terrorism is obligatory in Islam against the enemy of Allah (Al-Muhajiroun 2004n).

The devastation of Iraq has emerged as a primary aspect of the Islamist critique of Western states and indeed the global order. The Iraq conflict has also thrown into ever sharper relief the quandary of contemporary Western states in relation to their interaction with their Muslim minority community and especially those espousing an Islamist perspective. As has been seen, a primary focus of Western Islamism has been the inviolability of the *umma*. The attempt to inspire militancy through a focus on the suffering that defines the lives of many in the Muslim world is emerging as key component of the international

Islamist perspective. For example, the 7 July 2005 bombers cited the death and oppression of their Muslim kin in international contexts as a motivating factor in their terrorist acts against the British public. In Britain the challenge is the development of public discourses that acknowledge and allow for the often conflicted position of Muslims. Britain is actively involved in a military occupation that is directly responsible for the death of thousands of Iraqi Muslims and that has created the conditions for a descent into civil war in a Muslim majority state. This is a legitimate grievance. It is a concern raised by significant proportions of the British public on the basis of a shared humanity. However, the challenge to Western states is to adequately address the especially keen distress that many Muslims, because of an added sense of religious kinship, may feel about British foreign policy. The provision of citizenship and the rhetoric of social inclusion and validation of Western Muslims, when juxtaposed against the state's willing involvement in the perceivably arbitrary death and devastation of Muslims elsewhere are, for some Muslims, increasingly difficult to reconcile.

Importantly, the disillusionment with Western policy in the Middle East in this period was evident in a much broader cross-section of the Muslim community than the minority influenced by Bakri and al-Muhajiroun. Al-Muhajiroun seized on this common ground and attempted to link the concerns over the suffering of Muslims abroad to the socio-political experiences of Muslims in the United Kingdom. In this way, al-Muhajiroun attempted to universalise the imagery of Muslim suffering and affirm the need for a unified response. This aspect of al-Muhajiroun's rhetoric raised many difficult questions regarding citizenship. Denying the legitimacy of the nation-state and deploring the authority of the secular state over the lives of British Muslims, al-Muhajiroun essentially denied the concept of citizenship. To al-Muhajiroun the only affiliation a Muslim could hold was to the *umma*. This assertion, naturally, precipitated a need for al-Muhajiroun to rationalise and justify the presence of Muslims in the West.

Al-Muhajiroun attempted to prolong its own existence through the articulation of a 'covenant of security'. This formulation drew on the importance of covenanted agreements within Islamic theology and was loosely linked to historical experiences of Muslims in the early period.[6] For Bakri, with his radical rejection of the secular state in any context, the actions of a Muslim were governed solely by religion and its ability to regulate an individual's behaviour. In this conception, the 'covenant of security' was applied to forbid armed action by Muslims against their state of residence. Essentially, Bakri demanded his followers observe the spirit of the social contract between a state and its citizens, albeit reformulated in an Islamic format, while attempting to maintain his rejection the political legitimacy of the state. This concept also served a practical purpose. Al-Muhajiroun's continued existence was severely threatened by the possibility of a locally-launched terrorist attack. Any militant action by an individual affiliated with al-Muhajiroun would have led to the immediate outlawing of the organisation and the likely imprisonment of its members. In this way, the 'covenant of security' was advanced in a dual attempt to affirm the organisation's rejections of violence at home and to provide a buffer should such violence occur.

The underlying ethos of the 'covenant of security' was that the 'natural' state of relations between Muslims and the West was one of confrontation and aggression, a relationship that from the Muslim side could best be resolved through the recourse to jihad. To al-Muhajiroun Muslims in Britain, as a result of their Muslim identity, should have been predisposed to the rejection of the state and its socio-political norms. Thus, a covenanted agreement, as opposed to British law, was required to restrain Muslims from militant action within their state of residence (Al-Muhajiroun 2003e). However, even under the covenant concept, British Muslims were entitled to leave Britain to engage in jihadi attacks, even if those attacks targeted British troops. Essentially, al-Muhajiroun attempted to reassure the British public and media that it was not agitating for terrorist action within the United Kingdom (*Deutsche* 2003; Duguid 2003). Bakri frequently warned that the 'covenant of security' could be broken by either party. An individual Muslim could leave the state of residence, thus absolving him/herself of all covenanted responsibilities. The state, by failing to provide Muslims with the security of citizenship, could also be deemed to have broken the covenant, thus forgoing protection against internal attack. This conception of the relationship between British Muslims and the state was widely rejected within the Muslim community and its divisive impact is clear. Bakri, through propagation of the 'covenant of security', demonstrated once again his desire to drive a wedge of suspicion between Muslims and the broader community.

> For the moment Muslims in the UK have a covenant of Security that prevents them from attacking the lives and wealth of anyone here, however Muslims are also obliged to defend their life, honour and wealth when it is attacked and violated. With the worst housing, the highest unemployment, the largest number of race murders in Europe, a whole range of draconian laws tailored to intimidate the Muslim community, the Blair regime is today sitting on a box of dynamite and have only themselves to blame if after attacking the Islamic Movements and the Islamic scholars, it all blows up in their face! (Al-Muhajiroun 2003b)

The 'covenant of security' concept in reality was little more than a desperate attempt to retain the Islamist character of al-Muhajiroun within an increasingly difficult social and political climate. This is underscored by Bakri's commitment to his relationship with the media. Bakri had proved a popular target with the tabloid media—his willingness to issue controversial statements and his decision to live on state-provided welfare from 1996 proving excellent fodder (Richardson

2004:135–7). It was this very relationship, and the power of the media, which initially protected and yet eventually condemned Bakri. The media was also the vehicle that the mainstream British Muslim community used to confront al-Muhajiroun.

Muslim responses to al-Muhajiroun

In an interesting crossover to Bakri's position, prior to the events of 11 September 2001, an un-stated consensus was evident in which British Muslim leaders tended not to criticise 'or publicly disparage' other Muslims, even those representing fringe positions (Wiktorowicz 2005:59). This changed dramatically in the 'war on terror' era as British Muslim leaders grappled with the very real fear that minority perspectives, if left unchallenged, would be perceived as representative of a 'British Muslim' position. This consensus was therefore broken and British Muslim leaders spoke out regularly and forcefully against Bakri and al-Muhajiroun. As Bakri himself points out, it is of little concern to those espousing an al-Muhajiroun-style viewpoint what an organisation such as the Muslim Council of Britain thinks of their position (Bakri 2007).[7] Yet, what had changed was the willingness of all quarters to express their perspectives forcefully and in the mainstream media. It can be contended that this was in fact a positive, albeit unintentional, outcome of the presence of al-Muhajiroun. For the diversity of views that had been largely submerged in the media coverage of British Muslims in the 1980s was now, very firmly, on display. Despite this, for mainstream organisations al-Muhajiroun's ability to attract media attention and Bakri's deft handling of his own public profile constituted a major challenge.

The antagonistic relationship that al-Muhajiroun attempted to foster between British Muslims and the state triggered a severe backlash from the mainstream Muslim community. The oft-repeated assertion that al-Muhajiroun's penultimate aim was Islamic Revolution with the 'flag of Islam flying over 10 Downing Street' (*British Muslims* 2001d:3) was widely treated with derision. Yet, there was legitimate concern that such statements fed negative public perceptions of the British Muslim community. This was intensified by the media response that focused on the antics of al-Muhajiroun, often privileging their pronouncements and views over other, more representative, organisations. Among others, the Muslim Council of Britain was keen to expose the 'symbiotic relationship… between the media and al-Muhajiroun' (Bunglawala 2003:22).

British Muslim leaders repeatedly stressed the extremely limited and marginal nature of al-Muhajiroun and decried the sensationalism that appeared characteristic of the media's general response (al-Shafi'I 2003; Naseem 2003; Meo & Adams 2003:21). The perception that the British media was providing an inordinately significant amount of public space to the pronouncements of al-Muhajiroun is not without parallel in the history of British Muslims. As discussed earlier, the media handling of Muslim concerns in the 1980s provides a precedent. Similar to the al-Muhajiroun example, in the Rushdie affair minority views were often presented as reflective of a 'UK Muslim' position and moderate voices were sidelined by a media keen to exploit the tense situation. The al-Muhajiroun example suggests this trend continues and is largely attributable to the sensationalist nature of the tabloid media in the United Kingdom. As observers such as Elizabeth Poole point out, the British media's focus on the perceived threat of 'Muslim terrorism' spikes sharply after an international terrorist attack (Richardson 2004:130). Considering the rise in international terrorist attacks since the launching of the 'war on terror' this correlation has proved challenging for the British Muslim community.

The local Muslim community unequivocally rejected al-Muhajiroun as a negative or false manifestation of Islam. The perspectives presented by the organisation were fundamentally different from the mainstream interpretations of the faith. Nowhere is this clearer than in al-Muhajiroun's understandings of an individual Muslim's responsibility to undertake armed jihad. Instead of emphasising the differences between Muslims and mainstream British society, organisations such as the MCB focus strongly on the need for integration and co-operation. Al-Muhajiroun's response to the MCB was characterised by derision and charges of apostasy. This further revealed the organisation's divisive agenda and its embrace of the thinking of Islamist forbearers such as Qutb and Mawdudi. After the Rushdie affair, significant hyperbole surrounded the concept of apostasy in Islam. The Qur'an itself does not stipulate a punishment for apostasy. However, the normative historical response, supported by the scholars of the Classical period, was the death sentence. This was solidified in the Islamist revival period, with the rise of the Qutbian-inspired worldview best expressed by organisations such as Egyptian Islamic Jihad. In a more nuanced interpretation than carried in the tabloids, Bakri espouses a restricted view on apostasy, affirming that in the absence of an Islamic state, there can be no punishment for apostasy (Bakri 2007). Thus, Bakri claims, the ruling's only application in the modern context can be the exclusion of the apostate from the community (Bakri 2007).

The relationship between al-Muhajiroun and the MCB became increasingly confrontational in the post-2002 period. In early 2004, a series of police raids were held across the United Kingdom. In the aftermath, the MCB publicised its belief that Muslims should assist police in the common aim of rooting out extremists and protecting the United Kingdom from terrorism. Foretelling

Bakri's post-7 July position, al-Muhajiroun issued a press release condemning the MCB stance.

> So what can be said about those who contravene the Islamic texts and basic A'qeedah principles and take the Jews and Christians in the form of the British government and their police forces as friends and protectors over the believers, such as the MCB? Indeed to help and assist the Jews and Christians against Muslims in this war, whether it be the Blair & Bush regimes, their ministers, army or police is a clear act of apostasy.
>
> We have seen how the MCB are but a puppet organisation manipulated and controlled by their master Tony Blair [which gives] support and approval to the UK army to bomb, maim and kill Muslims in Afghanistan.[8]

The linking of the MCB's call for Muslim co-operation with authorities to combat terrorism in the United Kingdom with the British government's foreign policy in the Middle East went to the heart of the al-Muhajiroun doctrine. The apostasy accusation clearly demonstrated the organisation's determination to link the experiences of Muslims abroad with the lives and experiences of British Muslims. In supporting the MCB, and thus by extension the British government, al-Muhajiroun asserted Muslims were, in essence, endorsing the government's widely unpopular foreign policy. This position negated the lobbying undertaken by the MCB on foreign policy issues and obscured the MCB's willingness to differentiate between confronting foreign policy issues and endorsing the co-existence paradigm essential to the British Muslim community.

Al-Muhajiroun sought consistently to undermine the MCB and other mainstream initiatives, pointing out the pace of government level response to Muslim lobbying has traditionally been slow. In the aftermath of 11 September 2001 and the 3 September 2004 bombings in Spain, the British government intensified its engagement with organisations such as the MCB, a development that al-Muhajiroun ridiculed in its releases.

> ...one cannot help but laugh at the speed with which these initiatives have come about despite 30 years of useless pleading for race relation laws, better working environments and social and economic incentives for Muslims by the moderates (read non-practising Muslims here). A couple of rallies and demonstrations by a hand full of so-called extremists and one or two conferences discussing the real causes behind 9/11 and 3/11 and suddenly we find the Blair regime falling over itself to please the moderates lest the masses suddenly unite with these fundamentalists and turn Britain into an Islamic State!
>
> In any case the estimation of between 10,000 and 15,000 sympathisers for Al-Qaeda and the militants shows how little Blair really knows about the Muslims in his own back-yard. Even those who do not agree with what took place on 9/11 do not deny the sacrifices made by Sheikh Usama Bin Laden and the Mujahideen and their unflinching heroism against the terrorism and atrocities of the US and UK in Afghanistan and Iraq. Indeed one would be hard pushed to find a mosque

(among the 1,500 odd mosques) in the UK where the Friday prayers do not end with supplications for the Mujahideen fighting in Iraq, in Afghanistan, in Kashmir, in Chechnya and in Palestine and for Allah to give them a swift victory over the aggressors in those regions (Al-Muhajiroun 2004g).

The dovetailing of concerns regarding foreign policy and the fate of Muslims in conflict areas provides an interesting overlap between the radical and mainstream positions. However, while the concerns are clearly a commonality, the ways in which al-Muhajiroun and the MCB attempted to address such issues were diametrically opposed.

Situating al-Muhajiroun: the cases of Hamza and Qatada

Concerns regarding the proliferation of extremist viewpoints in the United Kingdom continued through the late 1990s and into the first years of the 21st century. In this period, al-Muhajiroun was usually presented as a vocal, yet largely harmless, minority group with little influence. However, other figures were attracting more careful attention. Omar Uthman Abu Omar, or Sheikh Qatada and Mustafa Kamel Mustafa, better known as Abu Hamza, played a central role in the Islamist networks in London. These men had been part of the mid-1990s arrival of a cohort of preachers that had entrenched the Islamist movement in the United Kingdom. Similar to Bakri, both men openly endorsed the concept of jihad, registered their support for bin Laden and agitated on behalf of 'Islamic' causes. British authorities appeared to struggle to contain these individuals and were hamstrung, in particular, by European Union legislation that demanded no individual be returned to a country where torture or execution was a possibility. Both men had loose links to al-Muhajiroun and were covered in the organisation's press releases. As these individuals came under more intense pressure in the post-September 11 period and were eventually detained by the state, questions were asked as to the similarities in Bakri's rhetoric and the differences in official response.

Sheikh Qatada, whose real name appears to be Omar Mahmound Uthman, is a Palestinian Arab who holds Jordanian citizenship. A veteran of the 1980s conflict in Afghanistan, he is understood to have met bin Laden in Pakistan in the 1989. Travelling on a forged passport Qatada arrived in the United Kingdom in 1993 and claimed asylum, eventually being granted refugee status. Underscoring the often murky links between British intelligence agencies and 'radical preachers' operating in the United Kingdom, it is alleged that during the mid-1990s Qatada met with MI5 regarding his ability to help 'prevent Islamic terrorism in the United Kingdom' (BBC 2005c). Active within local Islamist circles, Qatada came to public prominence in 1998 when he was found guilty on terrorism charges and sentenced to life imprisonment in absentia in Jordan.

Following this, Qatada came under intense scrutiny when recordings of his sermons were found in the Hamburg apartment rented by Mohammad Atta, the alleged ringleader of the September 11 attacks (CNN 2001). Qatada was arrested in 2001 under the *Anti-Terrorism Crime and Security Act 2001*, but released without charge (*British Muslims* 2001c:4). Qatada was rearrested and incarcerated in late 2001 as a result of new anti-terror measures that allowed the detention without trial of foreign terror suspects. After a two-year detention in Belmarsh prison, Qatada was released (but confined to house arrest) in March 2005 when a House of Lords ruling found his detention unlawful (BBC 2005b). The 2001 *Anti-Terrorism Act* empowered the British government to deport foreign nationals and an increasingly concerned public called for its application in this case. However, as mentioned, these powers were significantly constrained by Article 3 of the European Convention on Human Rights which precludes an individual's deportation to a country where the risk of maltreatment exists.

Qatada maintained a lower media profile than either Bakri or Hamza. However, according to international agencies he posed a much greater threat. German law enforcement documentation suggested that Qatada functioned as 'the mentor and spiritual authority for many militant jihadists, including the notorious Iraqi insurgent leader Abu Musab Al Zarqawi,' while Spanish investigations identified him as the 'spiritual guide of European jihadists' after the men involved in the Madrid bombings attempted unsuccessfully to contact him before their deaths (Bergen & Cruickshank 2005). Underscoring the official view of Abu Qatada, any kind of contact with him has been submitted in various legal proceedings as evidence of an individual's suspected involvement of international terrorism (Verkaik & Morris 2005). This raises interesting questions regarding Western responses to Islamists. Qatada's lower profile belied his influence and the level of his activism, while it could be argued that individuals such as Bakri merely pushed the debates which surround the Islamist worldview into the open.

Unlike Qatada, Abu Hamza Al-Masri functioned more as a caricature of Islamism within the United Kingdom. As leader of the Supporters of Sharia (SOS) a group that was aligned to al-Muhajiroun, Hamza shared Bakri's penchant for the media spotlight and was widely seen as a recruiter for al-Qaeda. A British citizen since the early 1980s, Hamza was influential at the infamous Finsbury Park mosque at which both September 11 hijacker Zacarias Moussaoui and the attempted shoe bomber, Richard Reid, were visitors (Bergen & Cruickshank 2005). Having sustained injuries allegedly during his time in post-war Afghanistan in the 1990s, Hamza was fitted with a distinctive false arm that the tabloid media seized upon. Hamza appeared to focus his international activities on Yemen, which requested his arrest and extradition in relation to terrorism offences. In 2003 the British government, newly empowered under *The Nationality, Immigration and Asylum Act,* which allowed the removal of UK citizenship from an individual with joint nationality if their activities were deemed a threat to the national interest, sought to move against Hamza. However, because of various legal technicalities, Hamza avoided arrest until May 2004 when the US unsealed a federal indictment requesting his extradition over the construction of terrorist training camps in the US, recruitment for jihadi activities in Afghanistan and attacks in Yemen (Whitlock & Schmidt 2004). He was arrested and released again in August 2005 and finally charged with 16 offences relating to terrorism and incitement to racial hatred in October 2005. With the conclusion of his trial in January 2006, Hamza was found guilty on 11 counts, including solicitation of murder and stirring up racial hatred. He is serving his sentence in Belmarsh prison. At the conclusion of his jail term, he may well face another trial as the US continues to seek his extradition.

These three men represented various elements in the Islamist movement. Indeed the distinctions between Bakri and his fellow 'radical preachers' are underscored by the differences in their current situations. In each case, the media's response altered significantly as the authorities and the public began to take the threat of local Islamist militancy more seriously. The tabloids, always willing to focus on the disfigured Hamza, initially presented him as a figure of derision. As Poole noted in her study of the British media this technique was regularly employed in relation to figures within the Islamist movement, with the 'extreme exaggerated for comical effect' (Poole 2002:149). The exception was perhaps Qatada who, as a result of the public and international link to al-Qaeda, was viewed as a legitimate threat to national security. Eventually, in Hamza's case, the comical appearance and the public bluster could not disguise the role played by his Finsbury Park mosque in Islamist circles and he was arrested and the media perception of him altered accordingly (Whitlock & Schmidt 2004).

In March 2004, Bakri's name was circulated in connection with a terrorist plot foiled by British authorities. It was alleged that several of the young Pakistanis involved had attended al-Muhajiroun meetings, although Bakri claimed they had quit his organisation finding it 'too moderate' (Bergen & Cruickshank 2005). The difference in official treatment of Bakri and his fellow preachers led to much speculation regarding his relationship with the authorities. The willingness and ability of al-Muhajiroun to publicly condemn the arrests of individuals like Qatada added to the sense of confusion felt by many, including the MCB. Al-Muhajiroun asserted that 'the detention of high profile clerics such as Sheikh Abu Hamza (and) Sheikh Abu Qatada is testimony to the anti-Muslim sentiment of the Crusader Blair regime' (Al-Muhajiroun 2004i). In addition, it laid the blame for these arrests on 'the Jewish lobby and the lackeys of the Blair regime within the Muslim community known as the MCB' (Al-Muhajiroun 2004h). By September 2004, 664 people, the overwhelming majority of them Muslims, had been held under the detention without trial clause of UK's new anti-terror legislation (Modood 2006:47). Considering the government's willingness to act against significant numbers of people, Bakri's freedom was difficult for many of his critics to accept. In what is perhaps a reaction to this, Bakri has since sought to draw some distinctions regarding his position. In 2007, Bakri self-identified as a 'radical' but denied the characterisation of 'jihadist', a label he acknowledged applied to Qatada (Bakri 2007). To Bakri, the categorisations are clear: what he terms 'so called moderates' minimise the militaristic connotations of jihad, 'radicals' engage with and legitimise the notion of militant jihad but within clearly defined circumstances and locations (which as a result of the 'covenant of security' do not include the United Kingdom) and 'jihadists' endorse militant jihad in any and all contexts (Bakri 2007). While evidencing some sympathy for Qatada, Bakri sought to distance himself from Hamza. Wiktorowicz makes the point that as a minority, within a minority community, the leadership options for the Islamist audience in the United Kingdom were limited (Wiktorowicz 2007: 142). This situation does, however, also make competition more personal, as a handful of individuals vied for attention from potential recruits, the broader community and the media.

In what is a recurrent theme, the supposed distinctions in the transmission of the Islamist perspective were increasingly submerged as the broader political situation spiralled towards binary interpretations. In the post-September 11 period and especially after the terror attacks of 7 July 2005, the political climate in the United Kingdom changed drastically. Preachers such as Qatada, Hamza and Bakri, previously tolerated, if not presented as objects of ridicule, became increasingly viewed as threats, even manifestations of a British policy of tolerance that had gone horribly wrong.

Al-Muhajiroun's downfall

The actual membership of al-Muhajiroun was always difficult to determine. Bakri made various claims ranging from 1,200 members (Rosen 2005) to 2000–3000 (Bakri 2007). Most academic sources placed the figure only between 50 and several hundred. All sources concur the dominant age cohort was 18–35 years. The British Muslim community exceeds 1.6 million. Considering this, even if Bakri's inflated statistics are accepted, the active membership of al-Muhajiroun was negligible and the publicity generated by the organisation grossly disproportionate. Wiktorowicz makes the point that al-Muhajiroun members were usually highly committed and undertook their public activism at a hectic pace (Wiktorowicz 2005). However, the profile of the organisation was clearly a stronger reflection of the strength of tabloid journalism. It could also be suggested that al-Muhajiroun served as a canvas against which the vital debate about Islamism in the United Kingdom could be played out. Moreover, the organisation's presence may well have revealed the increasing public and governmental concern over what al-Muhajiroun represented: the potential for extremist doctrine, radicalised by contemporary issues, to collide with concepts such as migrant displacement, socio-economic disenfranchisement, marginalisation and unemployment.

From mid-2004 onwards the pressure on al-Muhajiroun became immense, especially with the arrest of fellow 'radical' cleric Abu Hamza and the concurrent rise in questions regarding Bakri's continuing freedom. The organisation began to call itself Ahl us-Sunnah wal Jamaah, allegedly as part of Bakri's ongoing theological reorientation towards the Salafi movement. This decision may well have been more closely linked to a desire to deflect some of the media attention. The British authorities, empowered by changes to legislation, and a blending of public unease and media sensationalism, continued to increase the pressure on Islamist organisations. As a result, al-Muhajiroun's rhetoric became ever more strident. For example, in response to the changes to the citizenship process that included the requirement of the swearing of an oath to the Queen, al-Muhajiroun warned its audience that Muslims should refuse.

> The one who pledges to worship other than Allaah is not a Muslim, but rather a heretic and apostate (if he/she claims to be Muslim). This pledge shows the desperation and inferiority of the British government, by forcing people to become non-Muslims through declaring their allegiance to the Queen, may Allaah's curse be upon her (Al-Muhajiroun 2004b).

However, it was an international terrorist incident that provided the final catalyst for al-Muhajiroun's demise. The organisation's comments on the hostage-taking of children in the aftermath of the Belsen school siege were the final chapter in a long history of public agitation by al-Muhajiroun. On 13 October 2004, Bakri announced that he was disbanding the organisation. The rationale given for this decision was varied. Public pressure, the role of the media and the interest of the authorities all no doubt played a part. In the following months, media sources suggested Bakri had closed al-Muhajiroun as the result of a call by Osama bin Laden for Muslims to 'unify' in their conflict against the West (Faramarzi 2005). In 2007, Bakri focused on his reorientation as a Salafi and presented this process as a theological journey spanning the years 1999–2004. He states that the embrace of Salafi doctrine simply necessitated the closure of al-Muhajiroun (Bakri 2007). This is implicitly supported by Wiktorowicz who points out the 'Salafi ulama have widely and explicitly condemned the kind of activism and ideology proposed by al-Muhajiroun' as fostering divisions in the Islamic community (Wiktorowicz 2005:185).

Following October 2004, Bakri did not simply settle into a period of serene retirement. By January 2005, reports began to filter through the media that he had reengaged in new forums, including organisations such as the Saviour Sect and al Ghurabaa' (the Strangers). Moreover, Bakri was rousing the interest of the authorities by calling for jihad in various online sermons, including one in which he allegedly asserted that 'the Kuffar has no sanctity for their life or property' and encouraged people to become suicide bombers (O'Neil & Lappin 2005). Bakri's intensified use of the internet generated considerable interest because of the difficulties associated with tracking and monitoring his activities. This could be seen as a negative by-product of the organisation's demise, the increased reliance on the internet making the al-Muhajiroun-style message more difficult to contain. Yet, banned from mosques and without a clear mandate to lead an organisation, it appeared that Bakri was to remain a marginal figure on the far outskirts of British society. The terror attacks in London on 7 July 2005 propelled him firmly back into the media spotlight.

In the aftermath of the attacks, London reeled from the reality of 'home-grown' terrorists, young British Muslims with limited histories in the Islamist movement. Given his high media profile, it was not surprising that Bakri was raised as either directly involved or responsible for the establishment of the radicalised climate that produced the mindset behind the attacks. Back-flipping on the earlier tendency to revile him as a caricature, the media began to seriously question whether Bakri could in fact claim the 'title of the godfather of British terrorism' (Fielding 2005). The media rushed to resurrect an interview Bakri had given Portugal's *Publica* magazine in late 2004. In this meeting, Bakri had 'predicted' terrorist attacks in the United Kingdom. While on the surface alarming and utilised by some journalists as evidence of his high-level connections within international terrorist networks, this should be viewed with caution. Bakri had been unsuccessfully 'predicting' similar attacks since 2001. Considering the global security climate, the likelihood was that one of these predictions would eventually materialise. Bakri had also identified an organisation that he called 'Al-Qaeda Europe' as particularly advanced in the planning of terrorist atrocities against the British capital. In the aftermath of 7 July and following the claim of responsibility by an organisation calling itself '*The Secret Organisation Group of Al-Qaeda of Jihad Organisation in Europe*' this was further construed as evidence of Bakri's links to international terrorism. Once again, all things considered, Bakri's identification of a probable attack by an organisation with the oft-used term 'al-Qaeda' in its name was a relatively safe prediction. However, as the media and the public questioned the previous, now seemingly flippant, treatment of the domestic terrorist angle, the willingness to tolerate individuals such as Bakri quickly dissipated.

Bakri had an extraordinarily high public profile. His penchant for public activism and controversial statements has been noted. This said, Bakri claimed he had never broken British law, stating 'if I had broken the law in my speeches, why have I not been arrested and interrogated?' (Al Shafi'i 2005). This is a valid point. Even so, one would assume he would have been the target of significant police and intelligence surveillance. This suggests that any involvement in the attacks of 7 July was highly unlikely. In many ways, it no longer mattered. The advent of domestic Islamist terrorism decisively signalled the end of Bakri's tenure in the United Kingdom. The only question left was how the final act would play out. The British government's response, (potentially because of a lack of policy options) began to coalesce around the prosecution of clerics for inciting violence or through the application of seldom-used treason laws. Bakri, however, continued—either out of genuine belief or a wretched determination to cling to the role he created for himself as the 'extremist' voice of Islamism in the UK—to assert more attacks would follow. Furthermore, he condemned the subsequent MCB backed fatwa against terrorism as 'clear blasphemy against Islam' (O'Neil, Webster & Ford 2005). Perhaps most damagingly, Bakri also asserted that he would not inform British police if he did have any forewarning of a terrorist attack (Panossian 2005; Davies & Carlin 2005). In the post-July 7 climate this observation was destined to create outrage. In insisting upon this point, Bakri remained within the boundaries of his long-held contention that any alliance or relationship with a non-Muslim over a Muslim is 'an act of apostasy' (Bakri 2007). It is this worldview which informed the statements with which Bakri fell foul of the British media in the post-July 7 period. Bakri's stance, that if he received warning of another terrorist attack he would resolve it internally, perfectly blends the two fundamental attributes of his thought: the absolute insistence on his own power within Islamist circles and the belief that a Muslim's loyalty is to other Muslims exclusively. Yet Bakri's options were dissipating as Downing Street issued a blunt warning, 'let no-one be in any doubt, the rules of the game are changing', and announced tough new anti-terror legislation (Blair 2005). In the following days, hastily convened negotiations between London and Amman resulted in the signing of an agreement of understanding on human rights issues that paved the way for the deportation of Qatada, a development that placed further pressure on Bakri's position. Blair's proposed raft of legislation was extensive. The document called for the criminalisation of statements condoning or glorifying terrorism, the stripping of citizenship from naturalised citizens engaged in subversive actions, the exclusion of extremist preachers from the United Kingdom and the proscription of Hizb al-Tahrir and al-Muhajiroun (*Guardian* 2005). This final point, somewhat retroactive considering al-Muhajiroun's 2004 closure, clearly demonstrated the public desire for immediate and effective action on proponents of Islamism. To Bakri, the moves to deport Qatada were probably of much greater concern for they revealed that the British government was now determined to overcome the previous legal and political obstacles to remove or silence extremist clerics.[9]

Bakri's ability to continue his previous agenda in the United Kingdom was thus seriously curtailed. Reports suggested the Blair government was seeking to bring charges against him. These were flagged as including 'solicitation to murder, which carries a possible life sentence (and) incitement to treason and treason' (Townsend & Hinsliff 2005). In part, this can be dismissed as media hype as the applicability of treason laws, especially as Bakri did not hold UK citizenship, was highly questionable. However, that the emotive charge of treason was even raised demonstrates the public anger against Bakri at this juncture. Initially Bakri attempted to defend himself on the basis of his previous endorsement of the 'covenant of security.' However, he was increasingly trapped between the public desire for a clamp down and the British government's need to respond definitively to the attacks. The media began to focus on the previous links between al-Muhajiroun members and international terrorist activity. The most damning of these was an incident in mid-2003, when two British Muslims perpetrated a terrorist attack in Tel Aviv, Israel. Asif Muhammad Hanif and Omar Khan Sharif, the Tel Aviv bombers, were immediately investigated for an affiliation with al-Muhajiroun. Any operational or logistical role in the Tel Aviv attack was quickly denied, yet at the time both Bakri and Choudry issued public statements of support for the two men. Moreover, Bakri identified himself as the pair's 'spiritual adviser' (Fielding 2003). This information was not new; it had been covered and largely dismissed in the pre-7 July period. The advent of Islamist terrorism on British soil simply altered the equation. The level of public discontent with existing policy was articulated through the media and in online chat rooms.

> We are told that young Muslims are turned into suicide bombers by their 'alienation', 'discrimination', 'marginalisation' and a host of other sociological buzzwords designed to show that it is really our fault, rather than theirs, that they want to blow themselves up on the Piccadilly line' (*Sunday Business* 2005).

Bakri appeared nonchalant towards the public mood against him, stating in one interview 'they want to arrest me? Let it be. They want to deport me? Let it be' (Mekhemet & Van Natta 2005). In the end 'they' did not need to. In part undone by his own desire to be perceived as the voice of British Islamism, Bakri left the United Kingdom, via Heathrow airport, on 6 August 2005. Despite the political rhetoric, given that Bakri was *allowed* to leave this could perhaps be better understood as an official acknowledgement of his non-involvement in the events of 7 July. However, Bakri's situation in the United Kingdom had become untenable and the political rhetoric may well have been aimed at encouraging his flight. The media and the public were likely to continue to agitate for legal recourse. Bakri's departure simply removed the need for a difficult and high-profile trial which would only have drawn further attention to his views. Perversely, Bakri was protected by the very media mechanisms clamouring for his punishment. Despite the tabloid media's offensive against him, Bakri would have been assured that over the lengthy process of an arrest and trial the initial post-7 July anger would have quietened and the tabloid media would have continued to publicise his experience. For the authorities, this reality meant that trying Bakri would achieve little more than the provision of a strengthened and on-going platform from which to disseminate his views.

The British decision to allow, if not encourage, his departure suggests that for all the hype Bakri was an individual skilled at self-aggrandisement rather than a legitimate national security threat. Bakri, removed from the danger of prosecution, headed for Lebanon (where he holds citizenship) with the apparent intention of moving to one of the Gulf Emirates in order to continue his 'Islamic' duties. As was to be expected, Sir Iqbal Sacranie, the chairman of the MCB, applauded Bakri's departure, asserting that it 'will bring happiness and joy to the community' (Davies & Carlin 2005). Within a week of Bakri's arrival in Lebanon, the UK Home Secretary Charles Clarke, perhaps motivated by reports Bakri was planning to return to test the new anti-terror legislation, exercised his power to exclude Bakri permanently from the United Kingdom, stripping him of his residency status and ruling his presence was 'not conducive to the public good' (Ford & McGrory 2005).

Following this, al-Muhajiroun's former second in charge, Anjem Choudry, re-emerged into the media spotlight and claimed Bakri had been happy to leave, asserting he had only ever intended 'a stopover' in the United Kingdom (lse 2005). In a clear demonstration of the on-going determination to invoke the historical experiences of Islam, both Bakri and Choudry attempted to link Bakri's departure to the concept of *hijra*. Choudry claimed that Bakri was 'well-respected in the Muslim world [and that he was viewed as] a hero to Muslims around the world' (lse 2005). Nevertheless, Bakri was briefly detained, as a 'precautionary measure', within days of his arrival in Lebanon. After his release, Bakri claimed that persecution by 'the Zionist media in Britain' had forced the disbanding of al-Muhajiroun (Gillan 2005). In addition to this, the persistent rumours of his intelligence links resurfaced with internet news sites claiming, 'Bakri will serve as a useful MI6 asset in Lebanon by gathering Islamic radicals around him, with increased credibility among extremists for being refused re-entry into Britain' (Mathaba 2005). The role Bakri intended to play in Lebanon or beyond was no doubt interrupted by the outbreak of war between Israel and Hezbollah in Lebanon in 2006. At that time, media reports had Bakri attempting to secure safe passage from the stricken country on a UK warship, an accusation Bakri strongly denies (Bakri 2007). With his future unclear, Bakri's departure from the United Kingdom and the unwillingness of the state to allow his re-entry brought al-Muhajiroun to a conclusive end.

Al-Muhajiroun's legacy

Bakri's mid-2005 departure from the United Kingdom did not, however, signal the demise of the al-Muhajiroun perspective. Indeed, the validity of a study of al-Muhajiroun was underscored by the results of a December 2005 survey of 500 British Muslims. The minority appeal of an al-Muhajiroun-style position was affirmed as, when listed among a spectrum of Muslim leaders, only 17% of respondents cited any form of support for Bakri's teachings and views (27% cited disapproval). However, more startling statistics emerge in the age-bracket breakdown of results. As could be expected, the level of disapproval of Bakri's perspectives was higher in the older demographic cohorts. However, in the 18–24 age groups the level of support for Bakri's worldview was 28%. Put another way, of the 278 Muslims between the ages of 18–35 questioned in the survey, 54 people offered support or very strong support for Bakri.[10] This could be related to Bakri's media profile which, as a result of his ability to play the tabloids, was disproportionately high. Moreover, attitudinal data is notoriously unreliable. However, these qualifications aside, considering the general thrust of Bakri's worldview such statistics, when coupled with the continuation of terrorist activity inside the United Kingdom, demonstrate that the Islamist movement has retained its position in the margins of the British Muslim community.

The enduring relevance of Islamism was evident in the immediate post al-Muhajiroun period. Bakri had many years in the United Kingdom in which to develop his position and the two major heirs to al-Muhajiroun's ideology were the Saved Sect and al Ghurabaa' (the Strangers). Both organisations maintained websites reminiscent of al-Muhajiroun. The Saved Sect defined itself as the true heirs of the Islamic traditions of the Prophet and asserted its existence was required as 'the majority of Muslims living in the West are on the brink of committing apostasy (for example, by voting for man-made law and allying with the disbelievers).'[11] The website affirmed the Saved Sect was, rather than an organisation, a group of affiliated people working together. It also explicitly stated members were not followers of Bakri. Instead it presented them as the 'followers of the Saved Sect—the Messenger Muhammad and his Companions'.

Al Ghurabaa' (the Strangers) claimed adherence to the *Aqeedah of ahl ul-Sunnah wal Jama'ah,* the Islamic creed that al-Muhajiroun adopted in its final months. Al Ghurabaa' identified its purpose as carrying *da'wa* to the people and asserted that 'in this time of crisis...Muslims must unite their efforts and unify under one front against the Kuffar who have collectively launched a crusade against us.'[12] Again, this language directly correlated with Bakri's public statements regarding the demise of al-Muhajiroun. The al Ghurabaa' site tackled the question of Bakri directly, affirming that it was not a reconstitution of al-Muhajiroun and that the exiled sheikh had no leadership role in the organisation. However, the site did allow that 'many of its members are former students of [Bakri] and still hold him in very high regard'.[13]

The pains that the two organisations took to distance themselves from Bakri were unconvincing. The Saved Sect and al Ghurabaa' both emerged in the months following al-Muhajiroun's disbanding. The Saved Sect gained a public profile with a series of stormy protests aimed at discouraging Muslims from voting in the April 2006 elections. Prior to his departure from the United Kingdom, Bakri appeared to have been most closely associated with this organisation. In August 2005, *The Sunday Times* sent an undercover reporter to monitor the activities of the Saved Sect and published several damning accounts of Bakri's involvement. According to reports, Bakri and Choudry met regularly with members of the Saved Sect which was understood to comprise of a core of approximately 40 people (Insight 2005b). In the days following the 7 July bombings, Bakri was recorded by the reporter clarifying his public statements condemning the killing of innocents. In the presence of the Saved Sect members, Bakri asserted that while he condemned the killing of innocents, this did not include 'any Kuffar' (Insight 2005a). The apparent leader of the organisation, Sajid Sharif, allegedly an ex-al-Muhajiroun member, asserted that the 'covenant of security is broken and 'the banner has been risen for jihad inside the UK' (Honigsbaum 2005).

It appears the groups functioned interchangeably, Choudry moved between the two and the ethos articulated on the websites was clearly reminiscent of the defunct al-Muhajiroun. The Saved Sect website in particular bore a striking resemblance to the old al-Muhajiroun site. Articles posted online condemned democracy and integration. This agenda became even more evident in the aftermath of the Danish cartoon controversy of early 2006. The publication of a series of cartoons that were seen as vilifying the Prophet Muhammad galvanised Muslim communities throughout Europe. Once again, the nature of the Muslim response varied dramatically. In 2006, the political climate surrounding the 'war on terror' created a social context in which the Danish cartoons, and the decision of numerous media outlets to re-publish them despite the clearly articulated Muslim discontent, was seen by some as yet another example of the European disdain for Islam and Muslims. While mainstream organisations such as the MCB expressed their objections through the media, 500 people, apparently led by Choudry, gathered for a protest outside the Danish Embassy. Saved Sect members participated in this protest, many carrying placards urging violence and calling for a repeat of the attacks of 11 September 2001 and 7 July 2005. Choudry was arrested in March 2006 and charged with organising the protest, while Abdul Muhid, another Saved Sect member, was charged with the more serious offence of incitement to murder (BBC 2006). Choudry's case was heard in early July 2006, and he was fined a total of £800 for failing to give the appropriate notice for the protest, a result that prompted outrage (Taylor 2006). This outcome was also condemned by mainstream Muslims, who pointed out that the Saved Sect protestors were 'less representative of Muslims than the BNP are of the British people' (BBC 2005a). The protest was also rejected by other Islamist organisations, including Hizb al-Tahrir, and the Saved Sect hit back at the criticisms with distinctly al-Muhajiroun-style rhetoric.

> It is clear for Muslims to see that the European community have gathered together once again, as they have done so in the Middle Ages, in order to re-launch their crusade against Islam and its followers. Out of desperation to silence any person who exposes the flaws in their way of life, they are now unable to conceal their hatred for Islam and Muslims. Are a few cartoons really worth increasing the threat of terrorism? What will it take for them to learn that there is a very small limit in disobedience to Allah and it is only a matter of time before His punishments reach them and they are destroyed.
>
> The Western crusaders need to understand one thing: Islam is the future for Europe and the world and there is nothing any law, president, army, nation or people can do to stop it.[14]

The emergence of these two interrelated organisations was a clear legacy of al-Muhajiroun. The worldview articulated by both groups was reminiscent of the al-Muhajiroun position on democracy, international relations and the role of Muslims in the West. Bakri evidently functioned as the spiritual inspiration for these groups, with his former students heading both organisations and Choudry acting as a physical intermediary. Al-Muhajiroun was a marginal group and, as the organisation's legacy continues to splinter into different factions, it can be argued that these groups are likely to attract even smaller memberships. This will prove both a blessing and a curse to the authorities. In July 2006, a transatlantic investigation by the counter-terrorism unit of the New York Police Department estimated that al-Muhajiroun and its offshoot groups have between 600 and

1,500 members in the United Kingdom, and a further 1,500 around the world, mainly of Pakistani descent (Cobain & Fielding 2006). This includes a New York-based organisation, the Islamic Thinkers Society, which is understood as the reformulated US branch of al-Muhajiroun. The transnational reach of al-Muhajiroun, or more correctly the al-Muhajiroun ethos, was also underscored by the arrest in June 2006 of an American citizen of Pakistani descent who had become affiliated with al-Muhajiroun during a three-year stay in London. This person, Syed 'Fahad' Hashmi, was arrested boarding a plane to Pakistan and questioned by British authorities in relation to aiding al-Qaeda and delivering military hardware to militants in Afghanistan and Pakistan (Zambelis 2006).

In the United Kingdom, the Saved Sect and al Ghurabaa' were banned in late July 2006 under the newly expanded and highly controversial *Terrorism Act 2006*, which empowered the government to move against the organisations for the distribution of materials that glorify terrorism. As the source is US law enforcement, the agenda of this report should be considered. However, underscoring the continuing splinter effect, New York investigators released information alleging that al Ghurabaa', which had American branches had, by the time of its proscription, already formed 81 front organisations, support groups and affiliates in six different countries (Cobain & Fielding 2006). Such information draws into question the existing policy approach to Islamist organisations in the United Kingdom. The closure of al-Muhajiroun, while a symbolic victory for the Muslim mainstream, has clearly led to a splintering of its supporters. Moreover, the move to proscribe al-Muhajiroun was made only after its closure and this appears to have set a precedent. In the aftermath of the al-Muhajiroun experience, Islamists ensure their own survival by establishing a range of inter-linked organisations as a precursor to legal action against them. This dilemma has been played out at the highest levels and the most effective form of state response is still under periodic debate. Organisations such as the Association of Chief Police Officers asserted the risk of further underground proliferation should 'be weighed against the damage which these groups can inflict upon the communities in which they are operating legally' (Cobain & Fielding 2006). The divisive nature of such organisations is inarguable. However, the rapid splintering of al-Muhajiroun and the on-going disintegration of its supporters into smaller organisations does not benefit national security either. Indeed, the potential for individuals to move closer to an embrace of militancy is perhaps greater in this scenario. Similar to all terrorist activity, the events of 7 July 2005 clearly indicate that in the case of militant Islamism intent, rather than numerical strength, can be the most potent threat to national security. This was further underscored with the attempted attacks of late June 2007 in which the perpetrators were unknown in local Islamist circles. These factors combine to demonstrate that the al-Muhajiroun style perspective, as an example of Western Islamism, has proven a difficult and challenging force for both the British Muslim community and the state. The public space the British state was willing to allow for the propagation of Islamism changed significantly over the mid-1990s to 2005 period. However, al-Muhajiroun's closure and Bakri's departure clearly did not signal the end of Islamism in the United Kingdom.

Notes

1. Riaz Hassan (2007:22) interviewed 6,000 Muslims from Egypt, Indonesia, Iran, Kazakhstan, Malaysia, Pakistan and Turkey.
2. Anas al-Tikriti of the Muslim Society of Britain (Al-Hayat 2003).
3. Anjem Choudry, a lawyer in his 30s, joined al-Muhajiroun in the mid-1990s and quickly emerged as Bakri's right-hand man. He was sometimes reported as the United Kingdom Emir of al-Muhajiroun (Bakri is the Emir of the organisation worldwide) and functioned as the organisation's primary media contact (see Honigsbaum 2005).
4. Al-Muhajiroun (2004a) was at pains to draw distinctions within dar al-Harb; however, the basic two camp division was generally accepted in the organisation's literature.
5. For a detailed analysis of al-Muhajiroun's commentary on Iraq and Palestine, see Baxter (2005).
6. For a full exploration of the 'covenant of security', see Baxter (2006b).
7. In this study, the Muslim Council of Britain (MCB) is often referred to as illustrative of a 'mainstream' British community perspective, especially in relation to al-Muhajiroun. The MCB was established in 1997 and has over 400 affiliated organisations (Bungalawa 2005). However, it is important to point out that this group, while politically significant, is not universally accepted as a representative body. Indeed, the MCB's claim to the leadership mantle of the British Muslim community is disputed by various individuals, organisations and academics.
8. This declaration was issued by al-Muhajiroun (2004f) in conjunction with the Islamic Council of Britain, the Shari'ah Court of the UK, the London School of Shari'ah, the Society of Muslim Lawyers, and the International Islamic Front.
9. Qatada's fate is the subject of an on-going legal process. In February 2007 a UK court cleared the way for his deportation to Jordan. Appeals to this verdict are pending.
10. All statistics from Populus (2005:25).
11. Quote from the now defunct website www.thesavedsect.com, viewed 28.8.2005.
12. Quote from the now defunct website www.alghurabaa.co.uk.
13. Quote from the now defunct website www.alghurabaa.co.uk.
14. This text is from the article 'Hizb ut-Tahrir Fear Allah', which appeared on the now defunct website www.thesavedsect.com.

Conclusion

As a stand-alone organisation, al-Muhajiroun is unlikely to be remembered in the annals of Islamic history. The organisation, in both numerical strength and worldview, represented a fringe minority in a Western Muslim community. While it did endorse violence in the name of Islam, al-Muhajiroun was not involved in militant action against any state. The British government's plans to pass a retrospective ban on the organisation in 2005 were, arguably, more a public relations exercise necessitated by the July terror attacks than a meaningful political move. This is further demonstrated as the linked ban against Hizb al-Tahrir was shelved in December 2006 as a result of concerns that it would not survive legal challenge. Omar Muhammad Bakri's departure from the United Kingdom signalled the decisive end of al-Muhajiroun's tenure in Britain. Even al-Muhajiroun's subsequent splinter groups, the Strangers and the Saved Sect, were short-lived. The British authorities, empowered by a deeply altered political climate post-7 July, were more decisive with these smaller groups and effectively utilised new and expansive anti-terror legislation. During its lifespan, al-Muhajiroun functioned as an alternative to both the more established and international Hizb al-Tahrir tradition and the fractured, cell-based Islamist movement (both international and domestic) that still poses a significant national security threat to the United Kingdom. However, it also acted as a media-driven caricature of militant Islamism.

As it publicly eschews violence, Hizb al-Tahrir has been able to circumvent the British government's desire to force its closure. Al-Muhajiroun embraced a more militant interpretation than its parent organisation and endorsed violent jihad against the perceived enemies of Islam. Farouki (1995:39) identifies Hizb al-Tahrir as 'overwhelmingly premised on conspiracy theory assumptions'. The same was true for its splinter organisation. David Zeidan affirms the prevalence of the conspiracy theory mindset in the Islamist movement, stating proponents see their 'perennial enemies as the Crusading Christians, the Jews and secularism in its manifold manifestations' (Zeidan 2001:47–8). Al-Muhajiroun represented a uniquely Western manifestation of that tradition. This organisation can be understood as a moment in the on-going evolution of contemporary Islamism.

Since the time of Khomeini and Qutb, Islamism has been pushed and pulled between at least two competing trends: the inevitably nationalist orientation of a Khomeini-style revolution and the universalist underpinnings of Qutb. Al-Muhajiroun, while attempting to draw on the Islamist tradition, fitted neither. The organisation was clearly fanciful in its stated aim of enacting Islamic revolution in Britain. Moreover, the leaders of al-Muhajiroun, an Islamist organisation which operated in a secular, non-Muslim majority state had to employ significant dexterity to link themselves to the broader traditions that nurtured Islamism in the Muslim world. In this way, al-Muhajiroun became a hybrid organisation, a manifestation of 'dual incubation' which attempted to draw on the situational pressures facing the Muslim community in Britain and the external tradition of historic Islamism in the attempt to legitimatise its existence.

Al-Muhajiroun's short-lived experience underscored the obstacles associated with the propagation of an Islamist message in the West: the condemnation of the mainstream Muslim community, the scrutiny of authorities, and the often contradictory nature of the media's role. Al-Muhajiroun's experience also proved that while the Western Islamist path is difficult to tread, a minority will actively attempt it. This has been borne out by the on-going terrorist activity in the United Kingdom: the attacks of 7 July 2005, the attempted attacks of 21 July 2005, the alleged airliner plot of August 2006, the alleged plan to behead a British Muslim solider in February 2007 and the failed attacks against London and Glasgow in June 2007. Young British Muslims have played a role in several of these incidents. Despite the continued potency of the threat, the absolute fringe status of those involved needs to be kept in the strictest of perspectives. In 2004, the UK Home Office's *Draft report on young Muslims and extremism* asserted that only a tiny minority of British Muslims are involved in terrorism, either at home or abroad (UKFCO 2004). This reality is often obscured by several factors. First, while the national community and the Muslim minority community pay a high price, terrorist action does not require broad-based support. Thus the marginality of militant Islamists is not reflected in their capacity to cause damage to society as a whole. Second, because of the sensationalistic value of 'home-grown' terrorism in a context of vigorous public debate over minorities and the notion of national identity, the media portrayal of extreme viewpoints is not balanced *vis-á-vis* their influence. Finally, the difficult interplay between elements of an Islamist worldview and the views of the Muslim mainstream requires acknowledgement. Terrorism is deeply abhorrent to the overwhelming majority of people, Muslim and non-Muslim alike. However, the publicly stated grievances of the Islamist movement, especially in relation to Western foreign policy toward Muslim-dominated states, are shared by many in both the Muslim and non-Muslim communities. Put simply, despite the absolute rejection of the methodology of militant Islamists, elements of their worldview, such as concern over the fate of Muslims in Palestine, Iraq and Afghanistan, are shared by a much broader swath of the Muslim community and beyond. Many in the British Muslim community agitate for these causes, and the right to do so should be protected in a liberal democracy. These considerations suggest the need for a public and political willingness to engage with the some of the key perspectives of militant Islamism, while continuing to condemn the movement's methodology. In this perspective, the silencing of the proponents of Islamism may not be the most effective response. Naturally, this is a delicate process and the question of whether to exclude or include Islamist perspectives in political discourses is currently being played out throughout the international system. Nonetheless, the British embrace of liberal democratic norms marks it as distinct from many places in the Muslim world. One of al-Muhajiroun's primary objectives was to drive a wedge between Muslims and non-Muslims in modern, multicultural Britain. The presence of Islamists, many of which exploited Britain's open society, served this purpose as it contributed to a climate of fear. However, a shutting-down of the debate through repressive legislation, arrests and exile does not resolve this dilemma either.

The experience of al-Muhajiroun brought to light certain recurrent historical and political themes. The influence of the historical experience of the Middle East in the political formulation of contemporary Islamism and the question of parity of Muslims in the West are two examples. In the personage of Bakri, a stream of 20th century Arab political experience was revealed. Bakri, with his political activism, his affiliations, his expulsions, his migrations and his belief in the transformative power of Islam as a political doctrine, embodies aspects of the Islamist experience of the last two generations. His organisation, during its tenure in the United Kingdom, can be seen as one manifestation of a new stream of the evolutionary Islamist movement: Western Islamism.

The terrorist attacks of 7 July 2005 added a new urgency to this area of inquiry and provoked a more impassioned public discourse regarding Islamism in the West. At the centre of this narrative is the political doctrine of multiculturalism. Since the 1960s, multiculturalism has characterised the British approach to the changing ethnic landscape. Described by the UK Home Secretary Roy Jenkins in 1966 as 'not a flattening process of assimilation but as equal opportunity accompanied by cultural diversity, in an atmosphere of mutual tolerance', the right of immigrant minorities to maintain a distinct identity was enshrined within the British approach (Ansari 2004:209). The critical discourse surrounding multiculturalism and its implementation pre-dated 7 July, but it was forced into the public spotlight as a result of the attacks.

Britain provides an interesting example of a Western state's interaction with its Muslim minority. The majority of researchers interested in British Muslims and multiculturalism would agree that the legacy of the Rushdie affair lingers in localised disputes over faith schools, halal meats, workplace discrimination, and on a national level, the future of multicultural Britain. As Paul Statham notes, the challenges associated with race relations politics have become systemic:

> ...the state remains unwilling to recognize group rights for Muslims, fearing that their community associated activities will promote a political role for Islam that cannot be easily incorporated (Statham 2004:58).

The changing level of participation by Muslims in these equations is important. In the Rushdie affair, Muslim voices were often ignored. This is not the case in the 21st century. Muslim communities, advisory bodies, organisations and individuals have a presence in the political and public discourse of the state. In the realm of identity formulation Muslims, like all migrant communities, retain various individual, sectarian and national affiliations. The salience of these influences is undisputed. However, in the Muslim community, this can be overlaid with a shared sense of Islamic identity that generates concern for Muslim suffering elsewhere. The influence and strength of this concern is, at its core, individual and based on personal experience, political awareness, generational norms and religiosity. For some individuals, the impact this has on the notions of allegiance and loyalty implicit in and assumed by the status of citizenship can result in a disjuncture. Islamist organisations such as al-Muhajiroun attempt to capitalise on this sense of personal powerlessness.

Al-Muhajiroun, a Western Islamist organisation, was neither comfortably Western nor Islamist. The Islamist agenda of the organisation situated it firmly outside a purely Western paradigm. However, there are significant difficulties associated with the application of Islamist theory in the context of the modern secular West which complicate this as a comfortable categorisation. 'Dual incubation' is therefore offered as a term that can assist in the conceptualisation of the various socio-political and theological factors that may facilitate the growth of the Islamist movement in Europe. As part of this movement, al-Muhajiroun presented its political agenda of limiting Muslim assimilation and fostering transnational affiliations in the populist language of contemporary militant Islamism. This tactic assured the organisation highly disproportionate media coverage. This was further assisted by both the self-aggrandisement of its leaders and the political dynamics engendered by the climate of the 'war on terror.' In this conflict, hyped as a trans-generational war on terrorists determined to bring down an ill-defined 'Western' civilisation, the politics of fear have emerged as a potent tool for all involved. In this context, the threat posed by al-Muhajiroun was often greatly exaggerated. Al-Muhajiroun's grand-standing and media manipulation, characterised by grandiose calls to jihad and global Islamic revolution, entrenched these perspectives.

It has been the aim of this study to present an analysis of one Western Islamist organisation within its specific political, historical and cultural paradigm. The de-contextualisation of Western Islamist organisations leads only to an inflated and sensationalistic analysis of the threat they constitute. As Mazarr (2004:51) points out, far from being a unique and historically unprecedented threat, the Islamist movement requires contextualisation in a global history marked by violence. Mass movements, extremism and individual alienation are common historical themes and the organisations and national and transnational movements—Nazism and Communism for example—that have emerged in response are well documented. However, the ability of politicians or the public to maintain an objective perspective on the threat constituted by British Islamism has been clearly complicated by the experience of domestic terrorism. In contrast to the historical examples which were usually premised on an external threat, the challenge posed by militant Islamism is the idea of the potential 'enemy within'. The basic fact, demonstrated by the attacks of 7 July, that the few can damage the many, infuses any and all analysis of British, or indeed Western, Islamism with the emotive questions of national and individual security.

Yet the most basic challenge facing Islamists in the West is how to secure their existence in a cultural and political context in which they are broadly rejected. Ayoob (2004:2) asserts that the Islamist movement faces similar challenges in the contemporary Muslim world in which, despite its universal claims, it is usually tied to a national context. Ayoob's focus on the national orientation of contemporary Islamist organisations is not intended as an analysis of Western Islamism, yet such a categorisation can also be applied to al-Muhajiroun. Al-Muhajiroun, despite the rhetoric of universalism, was predominately a British organisation. It did espouse a global Islamist agenda and claim a limited international presence, but its theatre of influence and increasingly the issues with which it engaged (such as local elections, British politics and the role of Muslims *vis-á-vis* the state) were largely local or national. Ayoob (2004:2) asserts that 'the basic objectives of Islamists were and are to improve the quality of governance in existing states by making it conform to Islamic norms...These are national not universal goals'. Put simply, Ayoob argues that in the Muslim world contemporary Islamism has internalised nationalism and now works to effect change within the paradigm and confines of the nation-state. Islamic revolution in Britain was an impossible objective for al-Muhajiroun. Thus, it can be argued that al-Muhajiroun, like Western Islamism generally, is a new manifestation of the Islamist movement. Such organisations employ the traditional language, imagery and objectives of Islamism but as a result of their secular, non-Muslim contexts are limited to the endorsement or perpetration of violence as the only possible practical contribution. The glorification of violence has been a feature of the international Islamist movement in the post-Afghanistan period and especially during the course of the 'war on terror.'

Reflections on Bakri

Al-Muhajiroun's downfall was a result of numerous interlinked factors: public condemnation, British politics and media pressure. The media's role can be seen most clearly in the study of al-Muhajiroun's leader. Bakri's relationship with the media was marked by hyperbole. A skilled controller of his own public image, Bakri knew what the tabloids wanted. This was clearly demonstrated by his tactics, for example, in announcing the al-Muhajiroun conference on the impact of 11 September 2001. Bakri elected to call the event 'A Towering Day in History', well aware of the media storm this would trigger. The man clearly enjoyed the notoriety accorded to him by the tabloid press and saw the media as a vehicle through which to promote his agenda. In 2007, Bakri makes the valid point that if UK policy moved by *The Sun*, '[he would] be in jail' (Bakri 2007). British law may not move by the tabloids, but public opinion often does. In the end, it was the popular rejection of his presence and position which led to his exclusion from the United Kingdom. However, a more complex agenda than mere self-aggrandisement was evident in Bakri's use of the media. A phrase that appeared regularly in al-Muhajiroun's literature was the directive for Muslims to strike fear into the enemy's heart. It could be argued that Bakri literally used the media to achieve this objective. The British media was itself a player in this process and, as Wiktorowicz points out, Bakri's position with his intended audience was enhanced by his ability to offer an alternative perspective to both the national media which is seen as biased in its reporting on Islam and the mainstream Muslim media which is seen as compromised by its relationship to the state (Wiktorowicz 2005).

Al-Muhajiroun's leaders knew the organisation's profile was dependent on its ability to gain the lion's share of the media coverage devoted to this area of British politics. As many who have interviewed Bakri have noted, the man himself is charismatic. Wiktorowicz isolates Bakri's personal presence—his use of humor, his willingness to debate political issues and theological viewpoints and provide evidence for his positions—as the key factor which attracted young Muslims to al-Muhajiroun over other Islamist organisations (Wiktorowicz 2005). In this way, al-Muhajiroun, the organisation, was really about Bakri, the leader. In any study of al-Muhajiroun, Bakri's flair for showmanship emerges as the key factor. Despite a short tenure in the United Kingdom, Bakri displayed a keen understanding of the dynamics of modern, consumerist British society, and a willingness to provide the titillation that prior to 7 July 2005, sold papers. This is not to imply that Bakri is lacking in personal belief; rather it suggests that he fully understood he was on public display and, literally, selling a version of Islam. Moreover, it reveals he had a keen awareness that this version, his version, needed to compete in a marketplace filled with other organisations, both Islamist and mainstream, and the ever-present reality of dominant secularism.

Bakri himself seems to understand this relationship with the media as being a core component of his work, stating, 'God chose my enemies to spread my word' (Bakri 2007). In a clear example of his strong understanding of media culture in the United Kingdom, Bakri used the tabloids to speak directly to the British people. He did this in an attempt to present a confrontational vision of Islam and Muslims which served dual purposes. Firstly, by offering Islam as an oppositional identity structure it empowered those Muslims who perceived themselves as marginalised by British society and secondly, and perhaps more importantly, it made the integration sought by the overwhelming majority of British Muslims more difficult. In Bakri's mindset, in the long term, this only served his agenda. For if British society increasingly feared, and thus isolated Muslims, Islamism would have a more fertile breeding ground. Thus, Bakri's use of the media was designed to fulfill two key objectives: to publicise himself and his organisation within his intended audience and to influence the views of the broader community. Bakri was unapologetic about this, stating that his media presence enabled him to 'create fear in the heart of your community because you create fear in the heart of mine' (Bakri 2007).

This goes to the core of Bakri's agenda, the desire to see Muslims resist assimilation in the West. This agenda proved increasingly challenging as, while it is at times admittedly imperfect, an overwhelmingly positive process of integration continues. Muslim citizens of the West are navigating their societies, establishing their socio-political place, practicing their faith, raising their families and sharing in and contributing to the lives of their national communities. To Bakri, it is this very process of blending Islamic identity and life in the West which is to be resisted. While moments such as 11 September 2001, and to an even greater extent 7 July 2005 and the events of June 2007, place pressure on the British Muslim community, on a daily basis the everyday requirements of work, university and school bring people together. Bakri, losing the battle to insulate Muslims from their environment, used the Western media in the attempt to alienate the broader community from Muslims. His pronouncements were carried in high circulation tabloids such as *The Sun* and *The Daily Mirror*, thus a broad section of British society was encouraged to fear Muslims. As opposed to serious media sources, the tabloids were perfect for this agenda as both the journalists and arguably the readership preferred simplistic, ideally controversial, sound bites which Bakri was happy to provide. The climate generated by this tactic in turn made assimilation more difficult, even for the swathes of the Muslim community which rejected Bakri's agenda. This was, no doubt, the intention.

In the days following 7 July, the media, which had gleefully privileged Bakri's views on jihad, Muslims and the West, became the most vocal critics of his continued presence in Britain. Bakri was both protected and eventually dammed by his media profile. His departure from London was a result of his high media profile as a proponent of Islamism; yet simultaneously, the media presence he could generate rendered him inviolate from legal proceedings. In many ways, Bakri's experience mirrored that of the broader Islamist movement in Britain. In the pre-2001 period, Britain's relaxed approach to political dissidents fostered the emergence of an Islamist cohort. In the period between 2001 and 2005, these loose affiliations became increasingly scrutinised by authorities and, on occasion, the media. This led to a series of arrests of the so-called 'radical preachers', most notably al-Muhajiroun-affiliated individuals such as Qatada and Hamza. Finally, in the aftermath of 7 July, a concerted state and media crackdown against British Islamism occurred. This was evident in new legislation that was markedly more repressive than previous anti-terror measures, essentially a policy of 'zero-tolerance'. The outlawing of Islamist organisations that perpetrate or advocate violence is a necessary step for any government charged with the responsibility of maintaining national security. Yet the balance is a delicate one, with numerous tensions that require negotiation. In the aftermath of 7 July, the need for Britons—Muslim and non-Muslim alike—to confront home-grown Islamism was self-evident. In this context, the policy advocated by the state was a reasonable response. However, the potential to push Islamism further underground must also be noted. This was confirmed after the 2004 closure of al-Muhajiroun by the emergence of like-minded splinter organisations. Moreover, the current legislation, with its criminalisation of the glorification of terrorism, is problematic. Confronting and containing those individuals which perpetrate violence is a required duty of the state, the silencing of debate is not.

Utilising al-Muhajiroun as the vehicle for analysis, this study has offered an insight into those who struggle (or are unwilling) to reconcile an Islamic and a British sense of self. If the notion of 'dual incubation' is accepted then Western Islamism needs to be seen as a movement that draws on, but is different to, its Muslim world counterpart. The dissimilarities run deeper than geographic location. As al-Muhajiroun's experience indicated, the cultural and political milieu of a Western state is a difficult and inhospitable terrain upon which to project classical Islamist understandings. Thus, the doctrine propagated by such organisations is often a conflagration of Islamism, a simple glorification of violence, anti-Americanism and an anti-assimilationist mindset. Drawing a distinction between Islamism in the Muslim world and the West also suggests the need for different responses. The dominant Western response to Islamism in the Muslim world has, in recent years, been armed conflict. This will self-evidently not work in addressing the challenges posed by Western Islamism. Policing measures are a vital tool in combating physical terrorism, yet they do not in themselves negate the appeal of the Islamist movement. Indeed, al-Muhajiroun consistently pointed to the actions of the authorities, as they detained Muslims and searched mosques, as further proof of the anti-Muslim bias of the British government. This suggests that a more nuanced response to Western Islamism is required.

As Nilufer Gole (2003:18) has pointed out, 'contemporary Islamist movements are identity-building movements in the sense that they redefine, recompose and reconstruct Muslim identity'. This is certainly true in the case of al-Muhajiroun. While it remained a marginal and often sensationalised organisation, the ongoing and dynamic process of defining British Muslim identity was undoubtedly affected by its existence. This can be said for both the minority who supported its views and, perhaps more importantly, for the majority who rejected the Islamist worldview articulated by the organisation and defined themselves in opposition to such perspectives. In this way, the existence of organisations such as al-Muhajiroun served to sharpen the debate about issues such as religion, identity, multiculturalism and free speech in the United Kingdom. As this study has explored, a perceived and actual lack of socio-political parity between Muslims and non-Muslims has been a recurrent theme in the history of British Muslims. In the Rushdie affair it was a legal and social battle for inclusion and respect. However, the question now appears to be framed in more extreme terms. As the 'war on terror' continues, the question of the parity value ascribed to Muslim and non-Muslim life is increasingly raised. Despite the rhetoric for which his organisation gained notoriety, in an interview scenario Bakri is clear in his condemnation of the killing of innocent people (Bakri 2007). However, he refuses to condemn the killing of innocent Westerners without a linked condemnation of the killing of innocent Muslims.

This determination to link Afghanistan, London, Iraq and Madrid was seen as confrontational by many in the United Kingdom. However, it partly reflects the question of parity which infuses any study of the representation of victims of terrorism in the West and victims of foreign policy in the Muslim world. The challenge is thus to formulate national discourses which engage with some difficult realities. For example, while Western states insist on demonstrations of loyalty and assure local Muslims of their valued and important domestic contribution, the same structures are simultaneously involved in international military campaigns that appear to operate with a minimum concern for Muslim lives and safety. This was flagged in 2004 by the Home Office which pointed to a British Muslim 'perception of double standards in British foreign policy, where democracy is preached but oppression of the *Umma* is practised or tolerated' (UKFCO 2004). The report continues, citing a member of the Muslim Association of Britain, 'what is needed is a debate about the root cause of terrorism, which is our country's foreign policy. As part of a truly globalised community, many young British Muslims carry the burden of struggles elsewhere—Palestine, Iraq and Kashmir' (UKFCO 2004). The internalisation of this dilemma by even a tiny minority of Muslims, when added to the range of experiences suggested here—alienation, unfulfilled expectations, social dislocation and the tenets of militant Islamism—can have disastrous consequences.

The 2004 dissolution of al-Muhajiroun was a victory for mainstream Muslims in the United Kingdom, and no doubt a relief for authorities; yet the sentiments that the organisation expressed remained attractive rallying points for some within the Muslim community. The events of July 2005 made a powerful and tragic statement on the relevance of al-Muhajiroun's underlying themes. Islamist terrorism, when it came to the United Kingdom, arrived in the form of young British Muslims, exactly the people al-Muhajiroun had spent a decade attempting to influence. The presence of al-Muhajiroun and its various affiliates contributed to the political climate in which this attack was conceived. The period from the mid-1990s to 2005, characterised by a grudging and decreasing political willingness to tolerate Islamist perspectives, was decisively ended with the London bombings. Assisted by an outraged media, the British government demonstrated its determination to quash the ability of individuals to function as part of, yet in opposition to, British society. Bakri's role in this process was central. In 2007, in keeping with his self-identification as a 'radical' as opposed to a 'jihadist', he is quick to contest the decision to bar his return to London. The accession of the Brown government means that Bakri may well be making a play for a return to the United Kingdom. Indeed, provided the new incitement legislation is not applied retrospectively Bakri affirms he would return, at least temporarily (Bakri 2007). Moreover, he contends that through his exclusion, and the detention of the other Islamist sheikhs, the British Muslim community is now more vulnerable to the jihadist mindset. To Bakri, the government's response has only empowered jihadists in their critique of the West, providing them with the ability to point to his experience as proof that Britain refuses to 'co-exist' even with those who maintain a 'covenant of security' exists between Muslims and the state (Bakri 2007). In this way, Bakri argues that he was a 'cause of stability' for young Muslims in the United Kingdom, essentially acting as a prism through which the more 'radically' inclined Muslim youth could filter their intentions (Bakri 2007). Linked to this is the clear and self-assured belief that he, by virtue of his training and his position, would be able to alter their course. This is indicative of Bakri's understanding of his own role and importance within British Islamism.

Contrary to media reports, in mid-2007 Bakri claimed the 'covenant of security' was never broken in the United Kingdom (Bakri 2007). This assertion serves the underlying purpose of allowing Bakri to claim he never endorsed violence in the United Kingdom. Bakri strongly presents the 'covenant of security' as a binding Islamic doctrine. The covenant is forcefully presented as both individual and communal, with the arrangement covering the Muslim community as a whole and breaches of the covenant applicable to the individual's circumstances only. Bakri is even more pragmatic on this point, arguing that if an individual is arrested his covenant is broken but asserting that once the individual is released, if he makes the decision to remain within the United Kingdom, then his covenant is immediately restored. Moreover, according to Bakri, the individual aspect of the 'covenant of security' means a British Muslim cannot justify the use of atrocities abroad to justify acts of terrorism at home (Bakri 2007). Basically, in this interpretation, any Muslim who has lived, for any period of time, in peace with the community around him cannot engage in militant action against a local target. The attacks of 2005 greatly complicated Bakri's position. Indeed, this must have been an eventuality which Bakri, the 'radical' Islamist, had dreaded. Bakri's absolute determination not to condemn other Muslims was challenged as these young Muslims killed innocent people, an act which Bakri deems un-Islamic. Bakri, stuck between his refusal to condemn a fellow Muslim and the need to uphold the applicability of the covenant could only pass the opinion that these young men did not understand Islam (Bakri 2007). The nuances and intricacies of the various positions Bakri attempts to take are arguably lost on both a wider audience, and more damagingly, the audience which he attempted to influence. The crux of this debate probably lies in Bakri's personal circumstances. Bakri argues that as he was never arrested his own covenant with the British state remains intact (Bakri 2007). As, in July 2007, Bakri sits in a dusty outpost in Tripoli, away from his wife and children who remain in the United Kingdom, this pragmatic stance potentially leaves room for negotiation with the new British government.

In what appears to be further groundwork for a return to the United Kingdom, Bakri even asserts his exclusion is serving to damage the United Kingdom's national security as, in his absence, 'Sheikh Google or Sheikh Yahoo are informing Muslims that fatwas meant for Iraq or Afghanistan' are locally applicable (Bakri 2007). Even in this statement, Bakri's equivocal relationship to terrorism is clear. From a jurisprudential perspective, Bakri is drawing distinctions between what is allowed for Muslims living under a 'covenant of security' in the West and the permissibility of militant action in Muslim-majority situations marked by foreign occupation. Yet, in the all-important arena of popular opinion, he is merely endorsing violence. As the Muslim mainstream in Britain rightly argued, this is divisive. In response, Bakri's condemnation of what he terms 'so-called moderate' Muslims pivots on what he perceives as their selective application and engagement with Islamic principles (Bakri 2007). Bakri dismisses the Muslim mainstream in various ways, the most visual being the term 'chocolate Muslims', by which he literally means Muslims that 'melt' under pressure (Bakri 2007). By 2007, Bakri had stepped away from his previous criticism of specific organisations; again pragmatic reasons appear the most likely cause. But Bakri once again emphasises his own role. He argues that among the critical audience of young disgruntled Muslims disposed towards militancy, rulings from organisations such as the MCB, which exhibit the modernist tendency to minimise theological traditions such as the militant interpretation of jihad, carry no weight (Bakri 2007). Bakri contends that the mainstream's determination to adhere to modernist interpretations mean that its condemnations of militant action are, where it really matters, merely dismissed as a continuation of a pro-British stance. Bakri argues that his own condemnation of violence in the West, articulated through the insistence on the 'covenant of security', carries authority as he acknowledges the full scope of the Islamic tradition. In a linked point, Bakri—again speaking from exile in Lebanon—affirms that he was able to channel the discontent of young Muslims into demonstrations and conferences, the inference being that without his presence this tension will be channelled in more confrontational directions. However, when challenged, Bakri acknowledged that, in the case of the attempted terrorist attacks of June 2007, he would have been powerless to affect the plans of those involved (Bakri 2007).

This revelation highlights how the involvement of young, foreign-born Muslims, inactive in the United Kingdom's local Islamist circles, represents a new, even more challenging manifestation of the Islamist threat in the West. From what is known about the would-be perpetrators of June 2007, the likelihood of any of them turning up to an al-Muhajiroun-style event would have been exceedingly remote. The media focus on the amateurish nature of the attempted attacks also served to obscure the reality that individuals working alone and separate from the visible organisations are much harder to contain. In this way, a new phase of underground Islamism may yet prove a much greater threat than organisations such as al-Muhajiroun. These young men were adherents of the Islamist movement of which Bakri is keen to situate himself as part. In this way, June 2007 was perhaps an indication that Bakri's time had truly passed. It can be argued that any channelling of Islamist discontent which Bakri understands individuals like himself as having provided should be weighed against the publicising and entrenchment of the Islamist principles which cause such division, despair and violence.

Wiktorowicz, in an epilogue to his own text authored in the weeks following al-Muhajiroun's 2004 closure, opined it was unlikely that Bakri would moderate his views. However, he also intimates a story of a man caught in the rapidly changing political reality of the first years of the twenty-first century.

> [Bakri] does not necessarily support the tactics of al-Qaeda and its affiliates, such as beheadings and killing civilians, but when faced with a stark choice during a time of crisis between bin Laden and the infidels, he chooses bin Laden (Wiktorowicz 2005:215).

The same remains true in 2007, indeed if anything it is even more pronounced. As the discourse became ever more black and white, the room for movement and nuanced interpretation was hard to maintain. Bakri attempted to 'walk the line' in the United Kingdom and, as the situation spiraled, this was revealed as impossible. At the time, Wiktorowicz speculated that al-Muhajiroun's closure was, in part, due to Bakri's distaste for the 'almost myopic concern with jihad' which was becoming the norm at al-Muhajiroun meetings (Wiktorowicz 2005: 216). This perspective is supported by Bakri's disappointed observation in 2007 that al-Qaeda 'has permeated the hearts of Muslim youth' (Bakri 2007). The interplay between Bakri, al-Muhajiroun and al-Qaeda was a fascinating subscript to the organisation's lifespan. In response to al-Qaeda's April 2004 statement to the people of Europe, al-Muhajiroun asserted that bin Laden had emerged, like the 'true Lion of a man that he is, to speak with calm and tranquillity, as the voice of truth, and the champion of the cause of the Muslims' (Al-Muhajiroun 2004k). Arguably, as an Islamist organisation attempting to attract support within its targeted audience of disaffected young Muslims, al-Muhajiroun was obliged to issue clear statements of support for al-Qaeda. Moreover, a significant aspect of Bakri's thought is his determination to maintain Islamic unity, which he understands as precluding allying with a non-Muslim over a Muslim. This need to 'close ranks' is, one would have thought, secondary to the need to condemn the killing of innocent people, but within the current political context Bakri does not draw that conclusion. However, Bakri's personal perspectives on Osama bin Laden and the al-Qaeda operations may be more complex than the media (and potentially his own supporters) elected to present. Bakri understands his role as a theological once, arguing that his public statements are not his personal opinion. Instead, he contends he is offering an expression of the jurisprudential permissibility of actions and perspectives (Bakri 2007). Thus, while articulating a personal dislike for the tactics of organisations such as al-Qaeda in their operations against civilians, Bakri refuses to condemn them. This said, despite a media desire for black and white statements, Bakri has stated that the killing of innocent civilians is religiously prohibited. But, in the attempt to navigate the complexities of the current situation, Bakri displays a tendency to draw often problematic distinctions. For example, in relation to September 11, Bakri endorsed the attacks on the Pentagon (a military installation) as legitimate, yet he rejected the use of civilian airliners in the attacks (Wiktorowicz 2005: 64). This kind of reasoning did not endear Bakri to a Western media, or public, facing the very real threat of terrorism. As the 'war on terror' continued, this was compounded by Bakri's continuing determination not to condemn al-Qaeda. This can be attributed to three factors. Firstly, Bakri's longstanding refusal to condemn other Muslims. Secondly, Bakri presents himself as articulating statements of objective juridical opinion. In reality, this is greatly complicated by his concurrent political perspective and results in little more than confusion. For example, Bakri's equivocal stance is evident in the assertion that as al-Qaeda has called a defensive jihad, the organisation's actions are 'Islamically just within their own interpretation' (Bakri 2007). Finally, and potentially most influentially, Bakri is in a position where he is unlikely, unwilling and, in terms of the dynamics of international Islamism, potentially unable to condemn the activities of the most infamous contemporary organisation and maintain any form of legitimacy.

This leads into an interesting hypothetical. Given Bakri's determination to judge actions on the basis of Islamic permissibility, and his focus on the binding nature of the 'covenant of security', a declaration by al-Qaeda which specifically calls for Muslims in the West to attack their neighbours would place Bakri in a difficult position. When pushed on this point, it is Bakri's contention that such a declaration would force him to issue a condemnation of al-Qaeda as un-Islamic (Bakri 2007). The fallout of this for a self-styled 'radical Islamist' would be significant. The theological distinctions Bakri attempts to draw would likely be lost on the audience which he is attempting to influence, an audience motivated by political, rather than theological, considerations. Therefore, the bin Laden-style worldview can be understood more as an expression of political discontent than as a manifestation of theology. Bin Laden functions as a near mythic symbol of what is essentially anti-Americanism in the Muslim world. Rather than emulating or extending the theology of the 'revivalist' strain of Islamic thought in which he would no doubt situate himself, bin Laden's public position has focused on inherently political issues relating to his homeland of Saudi Arabia, the occupation of Muslim lands, a supposed conspiracy of the United Nations and the West, the arrests of Muslim scholars, corruption, unemployment, arms trading, economic boycotts and, of course, the need for military operations against both the Saudi government and the 'crusader' forces of the United States (Rubin 2002:137–42).

Bakri emerged as similar to bin Laden in his utilisation of the interplay of religion, politics, anti-Americanism and self-aggrandisement. The symbolism of Osama bin Laden, a man without classical training who became a figurehead of a movement of anti-Western sentiment, was of vital importance to al-Muhajiroun. However, like all things in Bakri's public profile, this was not static. In the pre-September 11 period, Bakri appeared happy to be linked to the al-Qaeda symbol. As the climate changed, Bakri distanced himself from bin Laden and denied having met the Saudi dissident. In an interview with Wiktorowicz in June 2002, this position was modified and Bakri claimed he briefly met bin Laden once in Saudi Arabia (Wiktorowicz 2005: 64). Yet by July 2007, Bakri was once again denying any meeting with Osama bin Laden (Bakri 2007). Indeed, on reflection, it could be suggested that the period of bin Laden's ascendancy was not altogether welcome for a preacher of Bakri's ilk. Bakri affirms that bin Laden has 'earned his right to lead' (Bakri 2007). However, from a theological perspective, men like bin Laden constitute a clear challenge to 'radical preachers' like Bakri who pride themselves on their Islamic credentials. Bin Laden's untrained status is, in many ways, an affront to the tradition of theological leadership in which Bakri is so keen to situate himself. Yet among Bakri's target audience, the attractiveness and power of militant action over theological leadership was becoming an increasingly important issue. As a result, Bakri was forced to dance an ideological jig around such issues. The bin Laden mystique is such that in a contemporary Islamist context, any other response (particularly a more theologically based one which would, in line with Islamic jurisprudence, likely be critical), risks revealing a more nuanced and complex message which is much harder to market than simplistic black and white interpretations. That Bakri, the man probably most closely associated with Islamism in the United Kingdom, would present al-Qaeda and its 'permeation of the youth' as a problem reveals much about the complexity of contemporary Islamism.

In 2005, Wiktorowicz pointed out that Bakri had tried to articulate a 'distinction between his personal feelings about [the killing of civilians and terrorism] and an *objective* jurisprudential position' (Wiktorowicz 2005:217). As Wiktorowicz rightly asserts, these nuances would be lost on most, arguably especially the young, religiously-unaware and often disenfranchised Muslims Bakri's organisation deliberately targeted. It was not Muslims confident or educated in Islamic traditions which al-Muhajiroun was seeking to influence. In the context of young British Muslims, caught up in the maelstrom generated by socio-economic instability, growing Islamophobia and the overlaid issues generated in a political era marked by Islamist terrorism and the 'war on terror',

Bakri's stance was either deliberately confrontational or flagrantly irresponsible. Indeed, returning to the contents of the al-Muhajiroun website, this point can be even more forcefully made. Bakri, in 2007, presents a nuanced interpretation of his worldview; he makes distinctions based on what is permissible within Islam and what he personally endorses. As the leader of an organisation and a mentor of young Muslims looking for answers, it was his responsibility to make these distinctions evident. However, the articles with which al-Muhajiroun transmitted its message often paid scant attention to these intricacies, especially in relation to global politics, an arena in which a reflexive assertion of militant jihad was the norm. Thus, the question of how Bakri was, and *allowed himself to be*, interpreted becomes significant. If Bakri does indeed subscribe to the perspectives he articulates in interviews with serious media sources and academics, then a brief survey of his organisation's own website should have informed him that the ways in which his targeted audience was receiving the message were markedly different. This is where the true culpability of Bakri's tenure in the United Kingdom is revealed. In the desire to retain the public profile he had created, Bakri personally contributed to a climate of hatred and fear which fed into the killing of innocent people. Bakri did this either out of an underlying belief in the jihadist mindset he claims to reject or out of a consuming desire to maintain his position, even at the cost of the simplification of his views to the lowest common denominator. While a more complex presence than the tabloid media allowed, Bakri was fully aware of the depiction of his views and did little to draw attention to the finer points of jurisprudence which he now claims continually guided his perspective.

Bakri, while engaging in nuanced debate over the technicalities, generally endorsed the principles of militant Islamism. As the situation has developed, he can do precious little to prevent the actions of those inspired by the worldview he endorsed. As Bakri himself points out, June 2007 demonstrated that the threat posed by militant Islamists is perhaps greatest not in the form of public organisations, but in those unaffiliated individuals whom have been inspired by its precepts. In this way, Bakri's continued relevance is limited. The movement to which he has dedicated several decades has spiraled into little more than the glorification and enactment of violence. For a man who prides himself on his understanding of the theological premise of the Islamist movement, this must be a bitter blow. This does not, however, mean that Bakri's Islamist career is over. At the core of his public presence is the directive which propelled him from Hizb al-Tahrir over a decade ago. Omar Bakri Muhammad seeks to blend belief with action. This is evident in his determination to re-organise in Lebanon with the establishment of the Iqwra Library for Reading and Scientific Research and a new group of students. The al-Muhajiroun experience has conclusively ended, brought to a close through a varied mixture of public pressure, media condemnation and theological imperative. For the United Kingdom, the battle with militant Islamism continues. It remains to be seen if the decision to exclude the public voices of Islamism help or hinder the process. For Bakri, a mixture of personal belief and an irrepressible desire for the spotlight suggests that serene retirement in Lebanon is unlikely.

Abedin, Maham 2004, 'Al-Muhajiroun in the UK: an interview with Sheikh Omar Bakri Muhammad', www.muhajiroun.com, viewed 15 May 2004.

Adams, Charles J 1986, foreword, in Jansen, Johannes JG, *The neglected duty: the creed of Sadat's assassins and Islamic resurgence in the Middle East*, Macmillan Publishing, New York.

Ahsan MM and AR Kidwai (eds) 1991, *Sacrilege versus civility: Muslim perspectives on The Satanic Verses*, Islamic Foundation, London.

Al-Hayat 2003, 'UK Muslim Society spokesman say Al-Muhajiroun statement on demos 'worthless', 22 November.

Al-Muhajiroun 2002a, 'Muslims to call for the destruction of the Jewish state', www.muhajiroun.com.

—— 2002b, 'Fascist Jewish state will never see peace'.

—— 2002c, 'Western values are perverted values', 24 October.

—— 2003a, 'Al-Muhajiroun, introduction to jihad part 1 & 2'.

—— 2003b, 'Al-Muhajiroun raided by Blair regime', 30 July.

—— 2003c, 'The Khilafah will return…', 14 August.

—— 2003d, 'Declaration from the conference on the Muslim hostages', 26 December.

—— 2003e, 'Aqd al Amaan: the covenant of security'.

—— 2003f, 'The policy of al-Muhajiroun in the West'.

—— 2003g, 'Saudi regime kill Ulema to please Bush'.

—— 2004a, 'Dar ul Kufr has divisions'.

—— 2004b, 'Our allegiance is with Allah not with the Queen'.

—— 2004c, 'Bombings in Islam'.

—— 2004d, 'Dar al Kufr'.

—— 2004e, 'Why have Muslims turned their backs on Palestine?'.

—— 2004f, 'Islamic response to the call by MCB to apostasies', 24 April.

—— 2004g, 'Blair contests the uncontestable', 2 June.

—— 2004h, 'Which do you prefer death penalty or life in prison?', 15 June.

—— 2004i, 'Recent arrests of Muslims in the UK', 11 August.

—— 2004j, 'Muslim demonstration shakes the heart of London'.

—— 2002k, 'A war for peace: an analysis of Osama bin Laden's message to the people of Europe, not the politicians of the West'.

—— 2003h, 'The tools and wishes of the Kuffar'.

—— 2003i, 'Muslim, British or American? A question of allegiance'.

—— 2004l, 'The Prophet Muhammad (SAW) is our example—did he ever vote?'.

—— 2004m, 'Jihad (the foreign policy of the Islamic state)'.

—— 2004n, 'Whoever denies that terrorism is part of Islam is Kufir'.

Al-Shafi'i, Muhammad 2003, 'UK: moves to freeze al-Muhajiroun as it prepares to "celebrate" 9/11', *Al-Sharq al-Wsat*, 8 September.

—— 2005, 'Muslim fundamentalist Bakri says he will leave Britain "Voluntarily"', *Asharq Al-Awsat*, 8 August.

Ameli, Saied and Arzu Merali 2004, *British Muslims expectations of the government*, Islamic Human Rights Commission, London.

Ameli, Saied, Manzur Elahi and Arzu Merali 2004, *Social discrimination: across the Muslim divide*, Islamic Human Rights Commission, London.

An-Na'im, Abdullahi Ahmed 2006, *Global citizenship and human rights: from Muslims in Europe to European Muslims*, speech, Netherlands Institute of Human Rights, Utrecht University, 10 May.

Ayoob, Muhammad 2004, 'Political Islam: image and reality', *World Policy Journal*, Fall.

—— 2005, 'Deciphering Islam's multiple voices: intellectual luxury or strategic necessity?', *Middle East Policy* 12(3).

Azzam, Abdullah 2001 [1987], *Join the caravan*, Azzam Publications, London.

—— 2002 [1984], *In defense of Muslim land*, Azzam Publications, London.

Bakri, Omar Muhammad 2007, Interview with author, Tripoli, Lebanon.

Batley, Brek 2003, The justifications for jihad, war and revolution in Islam, Strategic and Defence Studies Centre, Canberra.

Baxter, Kylie 2005, 'Islamism in the West: the life-span of al-Muhajiroun', *Journal of Muslim Minority Affairs* 25(1).

—— 'From migrants to citizens: Muslims in Britain 1950s–1990s', *Immigrants and Minorities* 24(2).

—— 2006b, 'Al-Muhajiroun and the covenant of security' in Mansouri, Fethi and Shahram Akbarzadeh (eds), *Political Islam and human security*, Cambridge Scholars Press, Cambridge.

BBC 2005a, 'Cartoon protest slogans condemned', *BBC News*, 2 May.

—— 2005b, 'Eight terror detainees released', http://news.bbc.co.uk/1/hi/uk/4338849.stm, 3 March.

—— 2005c, 'Profile –Sheikh Qatada', http://news.bbc.co.uk/2/hi/uk_news/4141594.stm

—— 2006, 'Two in court after cartoon demo', *BBC News*, 5 June.

Bergen, Peter and Paul Cruickshank, 2005, 'Clerical Error', www.peterbergen.com/bergan/articles/details.aspx?id=225#Thedangersoftolerance, 8 August 2005.

Blair, Tony 2005, 'Prime Minister Tony Blair's press conference', www.number-10.gov.uk/output/Page8041.asp, 5 August.

Bonney, Richard 2004, *Jihad from the Qur'an to bin Laden*, Palgrave Macmillian, London.

British Muslims (2001a), *Monthly Survey* 9(1).

—— (2001b), *Monthly Survey* 9(2).

—— (2001c), *Monthly Survey* 9(10).

—— (2001d), *Monthly Survey* 9(11).

Bubalo, Anthony and Greg Fealy 2005, *Joining the caravan?*, Lowy Institute, Sydney.

Bunglawala, Inayat 2003, 'Don't let the evil of extremism taint Islam's good name', *Daily Telegraph*, 17 September.

—— 2005, interview with the author, 28 June.

Cesari, Jocelyne 2003, 'Muslim minorities in Europe: the silent revolution' in Esposito, John and Francois Burgat (eds), *Modernizing Islam religion in the public sphere in the Middle East and Europe*, Rutgers University Press, New Brunswick.

Cleveland, William 2000, *A history of the modern Middle East*, Westview, Boulder.

CNN 2001, 'Q&A with Muslim cleric Abu Qatada', http://archives.cnn.com/2001/WORLD/europe/11/27/gen.qatada.transcript.cnna/, 29 November.

Cobain, Ian and Nick Fielding 2006, 'Banned Islamists spawn front organization', *Guardian*, 22 July.

Cohen, Ariel 2003, 'Hizb ut-Tahrir an emerging threat to US interests in Central Asia', Heritage Foundation, www.heritage.org/Research/RussiaandEurasia/BG1656.cfm, 30 May.

Cook, Yvonne 2006, 'Dr Muhammad Abdul Bari: taking a reasoned approach', *Independent*, 7 November.

Copinger-Symes, TR 2001, 'Is Osama bin Laden's 'Fatwa urging jihad against Americans' dated 23 February 1998 justified by Islamic Law?', *Defense Studies* 3(1).

Corey, Phillip 2006, 'Book ban anger: it will hinder freedoms', *Sydney Morning Herald*, 4 October.

Dassetto, Felice and Jorgen Nielsen 2003, 'Conclusions' in Marechal, Brigitte, Stefano Allievi, Felice Dassetto and Jorgen Nielsen (eds), *Muslims in the enlarged Europe religion and society*, Brill, Leiden.

Davies, Catorina and Carlin, Brendan 2005, 'Muslim cleric to seek sanctuary in the Middle East', *Telegraph*, 9 August.

Dekmejian, R Hrair 1994, 'The rise of political Islamism in Saudi Arabia', *The Middle East Journal* 48(4).

Denoeux, Guilain 2002, 'The forgotten swamp: navigating political Islam', *Middle East Policy* 9(2).

DES (Department for Education and Skills) 2004, 'Annual schools census, January 2004', www.statistics.gov.uk/cci/nugget.asp?id=963.

Deutsche Press-Agentur 2003, 'Britain pledges to help Israel trace Tel Aviv bombers', 1 May.

Devlin, John 1976, *The Ba'th Party: a history from its origins to 1966*, Hoover Institution Press, Stanford.

Duguid, Hannah 2003, 'Women: we want to change the world', *Guardian*, 30 June.

DWP (Department for Work and Pensions) 2005, 'Muslim graduates are missing out in the labour market' www.dwp.gov.uk/mediacentre/pressreleases/2005/jul/empl010-190705.asp.

El Fadl, Khaled Abou 1994, 'Islamic law and Muslim minorities: the juristic discourse on Muslim minorities from the second/eighth to the eleventh/seventeenth centuries', Islamic Law and Society 2.

—— 2005, *The great theft: wrestling Islam from the extremists*, Harper San Francisco, New York.

Esposito, John 1991, *Islam and politics*, Syracuse University Press, Syracuse.

—— 1999, *The Islamic threat: myth or reality?*, Oxford University Press, New York.

Faramarzi, Scherezade 2005, 'Radical cleric walks fine line in London sermon', AAP, 16 January.

Farouki, Suha Taji 1995, 'A case-study in contemporary political Islam and the Palestine question: the perspective of Hizb al-Tahrir Al-Islami' in Nettler, Ronald (ed), *Medieval and modern perspectives on Muslim–Jewish relations*, Harwood, Luxembourg.

—— 1996, *A fundamental Quest Hizb al-Tahrir and the search for the Islamic caliphate*, Grey Seal, London.

—— 2000, 'Islamists and the threat of jihad. Hizb al-Tahrir and the al-Muhajiroun on Israel and the Jews', *Middle Eastern Studies* 36(4).

Fattah, Hala 2003, 'Wahhabi influences, Salafi responses: Shaikh Mahmud Shukri and the Iraqi Salafi movement 1745–1930', *Journal of Islamic Studies* 14(2).

Fielding, Nick 2003, 'Passport to terror', *Sunday Times*, 4 May.

—— 2005, 'Terror links of the Tottenham Ayatollah', *The Times*, www.timesonline.co.uk/article/0,,2087-1706153,00.html, 24 July.

Ford, Rich and Daniel McGrory 2005, 'Preacher of hate is banned from Britain', *The Times*, 13 August.

Geaves, Ron 1999, 'Britain' in Westerlund, David and Ingvar Svanberg (eds), *Islam outside the Arab world*, Cruzon Press, Richmond.

Gillan, Audrey 2005, 'Bakri held as he leaves Beirut TV station', *Guardian*, 12 August.

Gole, Nilufer 2003, 'Contemporary Islamist movements and new sources for religious tolerance', *Journal of Human Rights* 2(1).

Guardian 2002, 'British Muslims', 17 June.

—— 2005, 'Full text-the prime minister's statement on anti-terror measures', 5 August.

Halstead, Mark 1988, *Education, justice and cultural diversity: an examination of the Honeyford affair, 1984–85*, The Falmer Press, London.

Hashmi, SH 2003, 'Interpreting the Islamic ethics of war and peace' in Hashmi, SH (ed), *Islamic political ethics: civil society, pluralism and conflict*, Princeton University Press, Princeton.

Hassan, Riaz 2007, *Inside Muslims' minds: exploring contemporary Islamic consciousness*, Brill, Leiden & Boston.

Hiro, Dilip 1989, *Holy wars: the rise of Islamic fundamentalism*, Routledge, New York.

Honeyford, Ray 1982, 'Multiracial myths?', *Times Educational Supplement*, 19 November.

—— 1983, 'The school attendance of British/Asian children', *The Headteachers' Review*, Winter.

—— 1984, 'Education and race –an alternate view', *The Salisbury Review* 6.

—— 1986, 'Culture and religion in a multicultural society: a dilemma for pupils', *Education Today* 36(3).

Honigsbaum, Mark 2005, 'Radical cleric leaves, but his legacy remains, *Guardian*, 10 August.

Husain, Mir Zohair 1997, 'The ideologization of Islam: meaning, manifestations and cause' in Jerichow, Andres and Jorgen Baek Simonen (eds), *Islam in a changing world, Europe and the Middle East*, Curzon, Richmond.

Idris, Sajjad 2003, 'Reflections on Mawdudi and human rights', *The Muslim World* 93(3/4).

Insight Team 2005a, 'Insider the sect that loves terror', *Times Online*, www.timesonline.co.uk, 7 August.

—— 2005b, 'Undercover in the academy of hatred', *Times Online*, www.timesonline.co.uk, 7 August.

Jansen, Johannes 1986, *The neglected duty: the creed of Sadat's assassins and Islamic resurgence in the Middle East*, Macmillan Publishing, New York.

Johnson, James Turner 1997, *The holy war idea in Western and Islamic traditions*, State University of Pennsylvania Press, University Park.

Joly, Daniele 1988, 'Making a place for Islam in British society' in Yngve, Tomas Gerholm and Georg Lithman (eds), *The new Islamic presence in western Europe*, Mansell, London.

Karim, Karim H 2002, 'Muslim encounters with new media: towards an inter-civilizational discourse in globality?' in Mohammadi, Ali (ed), *Islam encountering globalization*, Routledge Curzon, London.

Kelsay, John 1993, *Islam and just war: a study in comparative ethics*, John Knox, Westminister.

Kepel, Gillies 2003, *Jihad: the trail of political Islam*, IB Tauris, London.

Khan, Zafar 2000, 'Muslim presence in Europe: the British dimension—identity, integration and community activism', *Current Sociology* 48(4).

Khatab, Sayed 2004, 'Arabism and Islamism in Sayyid Qutb's thought on nationalism', *The Muslim World* 94(1).

Koopmans, Ruud and Paul Statham 2003, 'How national citizenship shapes transnationalism: migrant and minority claims-making in Germany, Great Britain and the Netherlands' in Joppke Christian and Ewa Morawska (eds), *Towards assimilation and citizenship: immigrants in liberal nation-states*, Palgrave Macmillan, New York.

Lewis, Bernard 1988, *The political language of Islam*, University of Chicago Press, Chicago.

——, *The crisis of Islam: holy war and unholy terror*, The Modern Library, New York.

Lewis, Philip 1994, *Islamic Britain: religion, politics and identity among British Muslims*, IB Tauris, London.

lexpress 2004, 'Muslim cleric says attacks on the UK inevitable', www.lexpress.com, 20 April.

lse 2005, 'Bakri will preach to Brits via the internet', www.lse.co.uk/ShowStory.asp?story=KI916354C&news_headline=bakri_will_preach_to_brits_via_internet, 9 August.

Mathba 2005, 'MI6 asset released in Lebanon', http://mathaba.net/0_index.shtml?x=304004, 13 August .

Mazarr, Michael 2004, 'The psychological sources of Islamic terrorism—alienation and identity in the Arab World', *Policy Review*, June/July.

McGown, Rima Beins 1999, *Muslims in the diaspora: the Somali communities of London and Toronto*, University of Toronto Press, Toronto.

McRoy, Anthony 2005, 'There can be no end to jihad', www.christianitytoday.com/global/printer.html?/ct/2005/105/22.0.html, 2 January.

Mekhemet, Souad and Don Van Natta 2005, 'Militant London sheikh had predicted more terror attacks', *New York Times*, 22 July.

Meo, Nick and Lucy Adams 2003, 'Jute, jam and jihad', *The Sunday Times*, 21 September.

Modood, Tariq 2003, 'Muslims and the politics of difference' in Spencer, Sarah (ed), *The politics of migration. managing opportunity, conflict and change*, Blackwell Publishing, Oxford.

—— 2005, *Multicultural politics racism, ethnicity and Muslims in Britain*, University of Minnesota Press, Minneapolis.

—— 2006, 'British Muslims and the politics of multiculturalism' in Modood, Tariq, Anna Triandafyllidou and Richard Zapata-Barrero (eds), *Multiculturalism, Muslims and citizenship: a European approach*, Routledge, London.

Munson, Henry 2003, 'Islam, nationalism and the resentment of foreign domination', *Middle East Policy* 10(3).

Naseem, Mohammad 2003, 'Muslim outcry at 9/11 March', *Birmingham Post*, 11 September.

NHSHDA (National Health Service Health Development Agency) 2001, 'Ethnicity, health and health behaviour: a study of older groups (summary report)', 1 June, www.nice.org.uk/page.aspx?o=501977nb.

Nielsen, Jorgen 1988, 'Muslims in Britain and local authority responses' in Yngve, Tomas Gerholm and Georg Lithman (eds), *The new Islamic presence in western Europe*, Mansell, London.

—— 1991, 'Muslim organizations in Europe: integration or isolation?' in Shadid War and PS Van Koningsveld (eds), *The integration of Islam and Hinduism in Western Europe*, Kok Publishing, Kampen.

—— 2005, interview with author, 1 July.

Nonneman, Gerd 1996, 'Muslim communities in the new Europe: themes and puzzles' in Nonneman, Gerd, Tim Niblock and Bogdan Szajkowski (eds), *Muslim communities in the new Europe*, Ithaca Press, Reading.

O'Neil, Sean and Yaakov Lappin 2005, 'Britain's online imam declares war as he calls the young to jihad', *The Times Online*, www.timesonline.co.uk, 17 January.

O'Neil, Sean, Philip Webster and Richard Ford 2005, 'Expect more bloodshed, says defiant Islamic cleric Bakri', *The Times*, www.timesonline.co.uk, 21 July.

Omar, Saleh 1996, 'Philosophical origins of the Arab Ba'th Party: the work of Zaki Al-Arsuzi', *Arab Studies Quarterly* 18(2).

ONS (Office of National Statistics) 2001a, 'Age and sex distribution', www.statistics.gov.uk/cci/nugget.asp?id=955.

—— 2001b, 'Country of British and national identity', www.statistics.gov.uk/cci/nugget.asp?id=958

—— 2001c, 'Ethnicity', www.statistics.gov.uk/cci/nugget.asp?id=957.

—— 2001d, 'Geographic distribution', www.statistics.gov.uk/cci/nugget.asp?id=956.

—— 2001e, 'Health and disability', www.statistics.gov.uk/cci/nugget.asp?id=959.

—— 2001f, 'Households', www.statistics.gov.uk/cci/nugget.asp?id=961.

—— 2001g, 'Religious populations', www.statistics.gov.uk/cci/nugget.asp?id=954

—— 2001h, 'The sizes and characteristics of ethnics populations of Great Britain', www.statsitics.gov.uk.

—— 2004a, 'Labour Market', www.statistics.gov.uk/cci/nugget.asp?id=979.

—— 2004b, 'Qualifications: annual population survey, January 2004 to December 2004', www.statistics.gov.uk/cci/nugget.asp?id=963.

Panossian, Joe 2005, 'Lebanese forces arrest Muslim cleric', *Guardian*, 12 August.

Parvin, Manoucher and Maurice Sommet 1980, 'Dar al-Islam: the evolution of Muslim territoriality and its implications for conflict resolution in the Middle East', *The International Journal of Middle Eastern Studies* 20.

Peters, Rudolph 1996, *Jihad in classical and modern Islam*, Markus Wiener Publishers, Princeton.

Phillips, Caryl (ed) 1997, *Extravagant strangers—a literature of belonging*, Faber, London.

Piscatori, James 1990, 'The Rushdie affair and the politics of ambiguity', *International Affairs* 6(4).

Poole, Elizabeth 2002, *Reporting Muslims: media representations of British Muslims*, IB Tauris, London.

Populus, 'Muslim Poll: December 2005', www.populuslimited.com/pdf/2006_02_07_times.pdf.

Qur'an 1989, *The holy Qur'an: text, translation and commentary*, translated by Abdullah Yusuf Ali, Amana Corporation, Brentwood.

Qutb, Sayyid 1978, *Milestones*, Holy Koran Publishing House, Beirut.

Radcliffe, Liat 2004, 'A Muslim lobby at Whitehall? Examining the role of the Muslim minority in British foreign policy making', *Islam and Christian–Muslim Relations* 15(3).

Ramadan, Tariq 1999, *To be a European Muslim*, The Islamic Foundation, London.

Rex, John 1996, *Ethnic minorities in the modern nation-state*, Macmillan Press, London.

—— 2002, 'Islam in the United Kingdom' in Hunter, Shireen (ed), *Islam, Europe's second religion. the new social, cultural and political landscape*, Praeger, Westpoint.

Richardson, John 2004, *(Mis)representing Islam: the racism and rhetoric of British broadsheet news*, John Benjamins Publishing, Philadelphia.

Rosen, Seth 2005, 'Imam's fiery message speaks to radical British Muslims', *Chronicle*, 17 July.

Roy, Olivier 1992, *The failure of political Islam*, Harvard University Press, Cambridge.

—— 1999, 'The crisis of religious legitimacy in Iran', *The Middle East Journal* 53(2).

—— 2004, *Globalized Islam: the search for the new umma*, Columbia University Press, New York.

—— 2005, 'Europe's response to radical Islam', *Current History* 104(685).

Rubin, Rubin and Judith Colp Rubin 2002, *Anti-American terrorism and the Middle East*, Oxford University Press, London.

Rushdie, Salman 1988, *The Satanic verses*, Viking, New York.

Sadiki, Larbi 1995, 'Al-la Nidam: an Arab view of the new world (dis)order', *Arab Studies Quarterly* 17(3).

Saeed, Abdullah 2002, 'Jihad and violence: changing understandings of jihad among Muslims' in Coady, Tony and Michael O'Keefe (eds), *Terrorism and justice: moral argument in a threatened world*, Melbourne University Press, Carlton North.

Sayyid, S 2003, *A fundamental fear: Eurocentrism and the emergence of Islamism*, Zed Books, London.

Shepard, William E 2003, 'Sayyid Qutb's doctrine of Jahiliyya', *International Journal of Middle East Studies* 35.

Siddqui, Kalim 1990, *Generating 'power' without politics*, Muslim Institute, London.

Spencer, Sarah (ed) 2003, *The politics of migration. managing opportunity, conflict and change*, Blackwell Publishing, Oxford.

Staloff, Robert 1994, *From Abdullah to Hussien: Jordan in transition*, Oxford University Press, London.

Statham, Paul 2004, 'Resilient Islam. Muslim controversies in Europe', *Harvard International Review* (Fall).

Stemmann, Juan Jose Esobar 2006, 'Middle East Salafism's influence and the radicalization of Muslim communities in Europe', *The Middle East Review of International Affairs* 10(3).

Sunday Business 2005, 'The challenge for British Muslims', 17 July.

Syal, Rajeev 2004, 'Cleric supports targeting children', *Telegraph*, 5 September.

Taylor, Ben 2006, 'Muslim cartoon protest leader escapes with £500 fine', *Daily Mail*, 5 July.

this is London 2005, 'London extremist flees to Beirut', www.thisislondon.co.uk/news/articles/PA_NEWA85768011123526141A0?version=1, 8 August.

Townsend, Mark and Hinsliff, Gaby 2005, 'Clerics facing new law jail threat', *Observer*, 7 August.

UKFCO (UK Foreign and Commonwealth Office/Home Office) 2004, *Draft report on young Muslims and extremism*, April, www.globalsecurity.org/security/library/report/2004/muslimext-uk.htm.

Verkaik, Robert and Nigel Morris 2005, 'MPs condemn house arrest and tagging plan to "control" terror suspects', www.globalpolicy.org/empire/terrorwar/liberties/2005/0127britlaw.htm, 27 January.

Vertovec, Steven 1996, 'Muslims, the state and the public sphere in Britain' in Nonneman, Gerd, Tim Niblock and Bogdan Szajkowski (eds), *Muslim communities in the new Europe*, Ithaca Press, Reading.

—— 2002, 'Islamophobia and Muslim recognition in Britain' in Haddad, Yvonne Yazbeck (ed), *Muslims in the West: from sojourners to citizens*, Oxford University Press, Oxford.

Weller, Paul, Alice Feldman and Kingsley Pudman 2001, *Home Office research study 220: religious discrimination in England and Wales*, www.homeoffice.gov.uk/rds/pdfs/hors220.pdf, Home Office Research, London.

Werbner, Pnina 1996, 'The making of Muslim dissent: hybridized discourses, lay preachers, and radical rhetoric among British Pakistanis', *American Ethnologist* 23(1).

White, Amanda (ed) 2002, *Social focus in brief: ethnicity 2002*, Office For National Statistics, London.

Whitlock, Craig and Susan Schmidt 2004, 'Vocal cleric arrested in London at US behest', *Washington Post*, 27 May.

Wiktorowicz, Quintain 1999, 'Islamists, the state, and cooperation in Jordan', *Arab Studies Quarterly* 21(4).

—— 'The new global threat: transnational Salafis and jihad', *Middle East Policy* 8(4).

—— 2003, 'Killing in the name of Islam: Al-Qaeda's justification for September 11', Middle East Policy 10(2).

—— 2005, 'Radical Islam Rising: Muslim Extremism in the West', Rowman and Littlefield, Lanham, Md.

WTR (World Terrorism Report) 2006, 'US Muslim Youths and Militant Islamism', www.stratfor.com/products/wtr/read_article.php?id=267746, 16 June.

Zambelis, Chris 2006, Arrest of American Islamist highlights homegrown terrorist threat', *Terrorism Focus* 3(25).

Zeidan, David 2001, 'The Islamic fundamentalist view of life as a perennial battle', *Middle East Review of International Affairs* 5.

Zubaida, Sami 1998, 'Islam in Europe', *Critical Quarterly* 40(1/2).

Islam and Muslim Affairs

A monograph series from the Centre for Muslim Minorities
and Islam Policy Studies, Monash University

Board of Advisors

Associate Professor Syed Farid Alatas
Department of Sociology, National University of Singapore

Professor Gary D Bouma
UNESCO Chair in Interreligious and Intercultural Relations – Asia Pacific
Monash University

Professor Howard V Brasted
Head of School of Classics, History and Religion
Director, UNE Asia Centre
University of New England

Professor Robert E Elson
School of History, Philosophy, Religion and Classics
University of Queensland

Professor John Esposito
University Professor of Religion & International Affairs
and Professor of Islamic Studies
Georgetown University

Professor Riaz Hassan
Department of Sociology
Flinders University

Professor Robert Hefner
Institute on Culture, Religion, and World Affairs
Boston University

Professor Michael Humphrey
Head of the School of Sociology
University of New South Wales

Professor William Maley
Director of the Asia-Pacific College of Diplomacy
Australian National University

Professor Abdullah Saeed
Sultan of Oman Professor of Arab and Islamic Studies
Melbourne Institute of Asian Languages and Societies
University of Melbourne

Professor Amin Saikal
Director of the Centre for Arab & Islamic Studies (Middle East & Central Asia)
Australian National University

Associate Professor Samina Yasmeen
School of Social and Cultural Studies
University of Western Australia